MW00713769

Scott Foresman

Science

See learning in a whole new light

PEARSON

Scott
Foresman

Editorial Offices: Glenview, Illinois • Parsippany, New Jersey • New York, New York
Sales Offices: Boston, Massachusetts • Duluth, Georgia • Glenview, Illinois •
Coppell, Texas • Sacramento, California • Mesa, Arizona

Series Authors

Dr. Timothy Cooney
*Professor of Earth Science and
Science Education*
University of Northern Iowa (UNI)
Cedar Falls, Iowa

Dr. Jim Cummins
Professor
Department of Curriculum,
Teaching, and Learning
The University of Toronto
Toronto, Canada

Dr. James Flood
*Distinguished Professor of
Literacy and Language*
School of Teacher Education
San Diego State University.
San Diego, California

Barbara Kay Foots, M. Ed
Science Education Consultant
Houston, Texas

Dr. Shirley Gholston Key
*Associate Professor of Science
Education*
Instruction and Curriculum Leadership
Department
College of Education
University of Memphis
Memphis, Tennessee

Dr. M. Jenice Goldston
*Associate Professor of Science
Education*
Department of Elementary
Education Programs
University of Alabama
Tuscaloosa, Alabama

Dr. Diane Lapp
*Distinguished Professor of
Reading and Language Arts
in Teacher Education*
San Diego State University
San Diego, California

Sheryl A. Mercier
Classroom Teacher
Dunlap Elementary School
Dunlap, California

Dr. Karen L. Ostlund
UTeach
College of Natural Sciences
The University of Texas at Austin
Austin, Texas

Dr. Nancy Romance
*Professor of Science Education
& Principal Investigator*
NSF/IERI Science IDEAS Project
Charles E. Schmidt College of
Science
Florida Atlantic University
Boca Raton, Florida

Dr. William Tate
*Chair and Professor of Education
and Applied Statistics*
Department of Education
Washington University
St Louis, Missouri

Dr. Kathryn C. Thornton
Professor
School of Engineering and
Applied Science
University of Virginia
Charlottesville, Virginia

Dr. Leon Ukens
Professor of Science Education
Department of Physics,
Astronomy, and Geosciences
Towson University
Towson, Maryland

Steve Weinberg
Consultant
Connecticut Center for
Advanced Technology
East Hartford, Connecticut

ISBN: 0-328-10003-X (SVE); 0-328-15673-6 (A), 0-328-15679-5 (B);
0-328-15685-X (C); 0-328-15691-4 (D)

4 5 6 7 8 9 10 V063 12 11 10 09 08 07 06

Consulting Author

Dr. Michael P. Klentschy

Superintendent
El Centro Elementary School District
El Centro, California

Science Content Consultants

Dr. Frederick W. Taylor

Senior Research Scientist
Institute for Geophysics
Jackson School of Geosciences
The University of Texas at Austin
Austin, Texas

Dr. Ruth E. Buskirk

Senior Lecturer
School of Biological Sciences
The University of Texas at Austin
Austin, Texas

Dr. Cliff Frohlich

Senior Research Scientist
Institute for Geophysics
Jackson School of Geosciences
The University of Texas at Austin
Austin, Texas

Brad Armosky

McDonald Observatory
The University of Texas at Austin
Austin, Texas

NASA Content Consultants

Adena Williams Loston, Ph.D.

Chief Education Officer
Office of the Chief Education Officer

Clifford W. Houston, Ph.D.

Deputy Chief Education Officer for Education Programs
Office of the Chief Education Officer

Frank C. Owens

Senior Policy Advisor
Office of the Chief Education Officer

Deborah Brown Biggs

Manager, Education Flight Projects Office
Space Operations Mission Directorate
Education Lead

Erika G. Vick

NASA Liaison to Pearson Scott Foresman
Education Flight Projects Office

William E. Anderson

Partnership Manager for Education
Aeronautics Research Mission
Directorate

Anita Krishnamurthi

Program Planning Specialist
Space Science Education and
Outreach Program

Bonnie J. McClain

Chief of Education
Exploration Systems Mission
Directorate

Diane Clayton Ph.D.

Program Scientist
Earth Science Education

Deborah Rivera

Strategic Alliances Manager
Office of Public Affairs
NASA Headquarters

Douglas D. Peterson

*Public Affairs Officer,
Astronaut Office*
Office of Public Affairs
NASA Johnson Space Center

Nicole Cloutier

*Public Affairs Officer,
Astronaut Office*
Office of Public Affairs
NASA Johnson Space Center

Reviewers

Dr. Maria Aida Alanis
Administrator
Austin ISD
Austin Texas

Melissa Barba
Teacher
Wesley Mathews Elementary
Miami, Florida

Dr. Marcelline Barron
Supervisor/K-12 Math
and Science
Fairfield Public Schools
Fairfield, Connecticut

Jane Bates
Teacher
Hickory Flat Elementary
Canton, Georgia

Denise Bizjack
Teacher
Dr. N. H. Jones Elementary
Ocala, Florida

Latanya D. Bragg
Teacher
Davis Magnet School
Jackson, Mississippi

Richard Burton
Teacher
George Buck Elementary
School 94
Indianapolis, Indiana

Dawn Cabrera
Teacher
E.W.F. Stirrup School
Miami, Florida

Barbara Calabro
Teacher
Compass Rose Foundation
Ft. Myers, Florida

Lucille Calvin
Teacher
Weddington Math &
Science School
Greenville, Mississippi

Patricia Carmichael
Teacher
Teasley Middle School
Canton, Georgia

Martha Cohn
Teacher
An Wang Middle School
Lowell, Massachusetts

Stu Danzinger
Supervisor
Community Consolidated
School District 59
Arlington Heights, Illinois

Esther Draper
Supervisor/Science Specialist
Belair Math Science
Magnet School
Pine Bluff, Arkansas

Sue Esser
Teacher
Loretto Elementary
Jacksonville, Florida

Dr. Richard Fairman
Teacher
Antioch University
Yellow Springs, Ohio

Joan Goldfarb
Teacher
Indialantic Elementary
Indialantic, Florida

Deborah Gomes
Teacher
A J Gomes Elementary
New Bedford, Massachusetts

Sandy Hobart
Teacher
Mims Elementary
Mims, Florida

Tom Hocker
Teacher/Science Coach
Boston Latin Academy
Dorchester, Massachusetts

Shelley Jaques
Science Supervisor
Moore Public Schools
Moore, Oklahoma

Marguerite W. Jones
Teacher
Spearman Elementary
Piedmont, South Carolina

Kelly Kenney
Teacher
Kansas City Missouri
School District
Kansas City, Missouri

Carol Kilbane
Teacher
Riverside Elementary School
Wichita, Kansas

Robert Kolenda
Teacher
Neshaminy School District
Langhorne, Pennsylvania

Karen Lynn Kruse
Teacher
St. Paul the Apostle
Yonkers, New York

Elizabeth Loures
Teacher
Point Fermin
Elementary School
San Pedro, California

Susan MacDougall
Teacher
Brick Community Primary
Learning Center
Brick, New Jersey

Jack Marine
Teacher
Raising Horizons Quest
Charter School
Philadelphia, Pennsylvania

Nicola Micozzi Jr.
Science Coordinator
Plymouth Public Schools
Plymouth, Massachusetts

Paula Monteiro
Teacher
A J Gomes Elementary
New Bedford, Massachusetts

Tracy Newallis
Teacher
Taper Avenue Elementary
San Pedro, California

Dr. Eugene Nicolo
Supervisor, Science K-12
Moorestown School District
Moorestown, New Jersey

Jeffrey Pastrak
School District of Philadelphia
Philadelphia, Pennsylvania

Helen Pedigo
Teacher
Mt. Carmel Elementary
Huntsville Alabama

Becky Peltonen
Teacher
Patterson Elementary School
Panama City, Florida

Sherri Pensler
Teacher/ESOL
Claude Pepper Elementary
Miami, Florida

Virginia Rogliano
Teacher
Bridgeview Elementary
South Charleston, West
Virginia

Debbie Sanders
Teacher
Thunderbolt Elementary
Orange Park, Florida

Grethel Santamarina
Teacher
E.W.F. Stirrup School
Miami, Florida

Migdalia Schneider
Teacher/Bilingual
Lindell School
Long Beach, New York

Susan Shelly
Teacher
Bonita Springs Elementary
Bonita Springs, Florida

Peggy Terry
Teacher
Madison District 151
South Holland, Illinois

Jane M. Thompson
Teacher
Emma Ward Elementary
Lawrenceburg, Kentucky

Martha Todd
Teacher
W. H. Rhodes Elementary
Milton, Florida

Renee Williams
Teacher
Central Elementary
Bloomfield, New Mexico

Myra Wood
Teacher
Madison Street Academy
Ocala, Florida

Marion Zampa
Teacher
Shawnee Mission
School District
Overland Park, Kansas

Science

See learning in a whole new light

Unit A Life Science

How do the different parts of a plant help it live and grow?

Chapter 1 • Plants and How They Grow

Chapter 2 • How Animals Live

How do different animals live, grow, and change?

Unit A Life Science

How are ecosystems different from each other?

Chapter 3 • Where Plants and Animals Live

Chapter 4 • Plants and Animals Living Together

How do plants and animals interact?

Unit B Earth Science

How does water change form?

How does weather follow patterns?

Chapter 7 • Rocks and Soil

Why are rocks and soil important resources?

Unit B Earth Science

How do forces cause changes on Earth's surface?

Chapter 8 • Changes on Earth

Chapter 9 • Natural Resources

**How can people
use natural
resources
responsibly?**

Unit C Physical Science

What are the properties of matter?

What are physical and chemical changes in matter?

Chapter 12 • Forces and Motion

How do forces cause motion and get work done?

Unit C Physical Science

How does energy change form?

Chapter 13 • Energy

Chapter 14 • Sound

How does energy produce the sounds we hear?

Unit D Space and Technology

What patterns do the Earth, Sun, Moon, and stars show?

How are the planets in the solar system alike and different?

Chapter 17 • Science in Our Lives

How does technology affect our lives?

How to Read Science

A page like the one below is found near the beginning of each chapter. It shows you how to use a reading skill that will help you understand what you read.

Before Reading

Before you read the chapter, read the Build Background page and think about how to answer the question. Recall what you already know as you answer the question. Work with a partner to make a list of what you already know. Then read the How to Read Science page.

Target Reading Skill
Each page has one target reading skill. The reading skill corresponds with a process skill in the Directed Inquiry activity on the facing page. The reading skill will be useful as you read science.

Real-World Connection
Each page has an example of something you might read. It also connects with the Directed Inquiry activity.

Graphic Organizer
A useful strategy for understanding anything you read is to make a graphic organizer. A graphic organizer can help you think about the information and how parts of it relate to each other. Each reading skill has a graphic organizer.

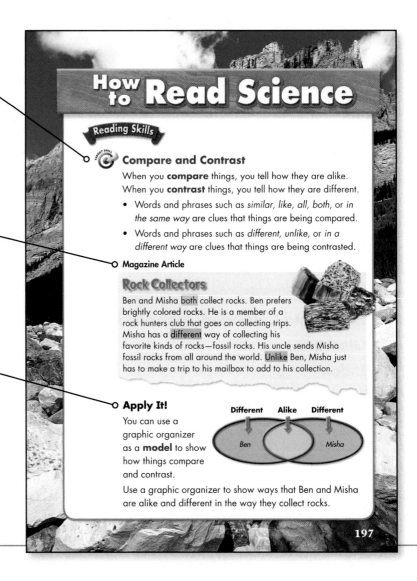

How to Read Science

Reading Skills

Compare and Contrast
When you **compare** things, you tell how they are alike. When you **contrast** things, you tell how they are different.
- Words and phrases such as *similar, like, all, both,* or *in the same way* are clues that things are being compared.
- Words and phrases such as *different, unlike,* or *in a different way* are clues that things are being contrasted.

Magazine Article

Rock Collectors

Ben and Misha both collect rocks. Ben prefers brightly colored rocks. He is a member of a rock hunters club that goes on collecting trips. Misha has a different way of collecting his favorite kinds of rocks—fossil rocks. His uncle sends Misha fossil rocks from all around the world. Unlike Ben, Misha just has to make a trip to his mailbox to add to his collection.

Apply It!
You can use a graphic organizer as a **model** to show how things compare and contrast.

Different   Alike   Different

Ben   Misha

Use a graphic organizer to show ways that Ben and Misha are alike and different in the way they collect rocks.

197

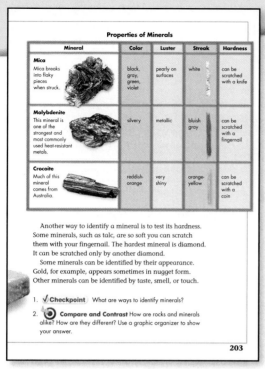

Properties of Minerals

Mineral	Color	Luster	Streak	Hardness
Mica Mica breaks into flaky pieces when struck.	black, gray, green, violet	pearly on surfaces	white	can be scratched with a knife
Molybdenite This mineral is one of the strongest and most commonly used heat-resistant metals.	silvery	metallic	bluish gray	can be scratched with a fingernail
Crocoite Much of this mineral comes from Australia.	reddish-orange	very shiny	orange-yellow	can be scratched with a coin

Another way to identify a mineral is to test its hardness. Some minerals, such as talc, are so soft you can scratch them with your fingernail. The hardest mineral is diamond. It can be scratched only by another diamond.

Some minerals can be identified by their appearance. Gold, for example, appears sometimes in nugget form. Other minerals can be identified by taste, smell, or touch.

1. ✓ **Checkpoint** What are ways to identify minerals?

2.  **Compare and Contrast** How are rocks and minerals alike? How are they different? Use a graphic organizer to show your answer.

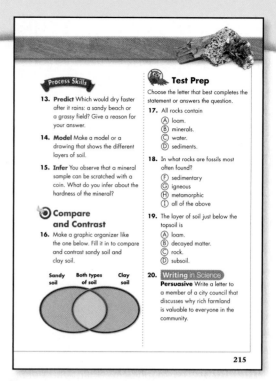

Process Skills

13. **Predict** Which would dry faster after it rains: a sandy beach or a grassy field? Give a reason for your answer.

14. **Model** Make a model or a drawing that shows the different layers of soil.

15. **Infer** You observe that a mineral sample can be scratched with a coin. What do you infer about the hardness of the mineral?

Compare and Contrast

16. Make a graphic organizer like the one below. Fill it in to compare and contrast sandy soil and clay soil.

Sandy soil   Both types of soil   Clay soil

Test Prep

Choose the letter that best completes the statement or answers the question.

17. All rocks contain
  Ⓐ loam.
  Ⓑ minerals.
  Ⓒ water.
  Ⓓ sediments.

18. In what rocks are fossils most often found?
  Ⓕ sedimentary
  Ⓖ igneous
  Ⓗ metamorphic
  Ⓘ all of the above

19. The layer of soil just below the topsoil is
  Ⓐ loam.
  Ⓑ decayed matter.
  Ⓒ rock.
  Ⓓ subsoil.

20. **Writing in Science**
  Persuasive Write a letter to a member of a city council that discusses why rich farmland is valuable to everyone in the community.

During Reading

As you read the lesson, use the Checkpoint to check your understanding. Some checkpoints ask you to use the target reading skill.

After Reading

After you have read the chapter, think about what you found out. Exchange ideas with a partner. Compare the list you made before you read the chapter with what you learned by reading it. Answer the questions in the Chapter Review. One question uses the target reading skill.

Graphic Organizers

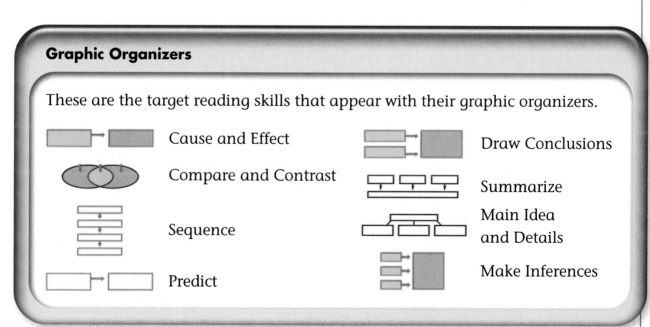

These are the target reading skills that appear with their graphic organizers.

Cause and Effect

Compare and Contrast

Sequence

Predict

Draw Conclusions

Summarize

Main Idea and Details

Make Inferences

Science Process Skills

Investigating Weather

Scientists use process skills when they investigate places or events. You will use these skills when you do the activities in this book. Which process skills might scientists use when they investigate weather?

Observe

A scientist who studies weather observes many things. You use your senses too to find out about other objects, events, or living things.

Classify

Scientists classify clouds according to their properties. When you classify, you arrange or sort objects, events, or living things.

Estimate and Measure

Scientists estimate how much rain will fall. Then they use tools to measure how much rain fell.

Infer
Scientists infer what they think is happening during a storm, based on what they already know.

Predict
Scientists predict how weather will change. Then people know how to get ready for the change.

Make and Use Models
Scientists make and use models such as pictures and maps. Models are like real events in some ways, but are different in other ways.

Make Operational Definitions
Scientists can use what they know to make operational definitions about what they observe during a storm.

Science Process Skills

Form Questions and Hypotheses

Think of a statement that you can test to solve a problem or answer a question about storms or other kinds of weather.

Investigate and Experiment

As scientists observe storms, they investigate and experiment to test a hypothesis.

Identify and Control Variables

As scientists perform an experiment, they identify and control the variables so that they test only one thing at a time.

If you were a scientist, you might want to learn more about storms. What questions might you have about storms? How would you use process skills in your investigation?

Collect Data
Scientists collect data from their observations of weather. They put the data into charts or tables.

Interpret Data
Scientists use the information they collected to solve problems or answer questions.

Communicate
Scientists use words, pictures, charts, and graphs to share information about their investigation.

Using Scientific Methods for Science Inquiry

Scientists use scientific methods as they work. Scientific methods are organized ways to answer questions and solve problems. Scientific methods include the steps shown here. Scientists might not use all the steps. They might not use the steps in this order. You will use scientific methods when you do the **Full Inquiry** activity at the end of each unit. You also will use scientific methods when you do Science Fair Projects.

Ask a question.

You might have a question about something you observe.

What material is best for keeping heat in water?

State your hypothesis.

A hypothesis is a possible answer to your question.

If I wrap the jar in fake fur, then the water will stay warm the longest.

Identify and control variables.

Variables are things that can change. For a fair test, you choose just one variable to change. Keep all other variables the same.

Test other materials. Put the same amount of warm water in other jars that are the same size and shape.

Test your hypothesis.

Make a plan to test your hypothesis. Collect materials and tools. Then follow your plan.

Collect and record your data.

Keep good records of what you do and find out. Use tables and pictures to help.

Interpret your data.

Organize your notes and records to make them clear. Make diagrams, charts, or graphs to help.

State your conclusion.

Your conclusion is a decision you make based on your data. Communicate what you found out. Tell whether or not your data supported your hypothesis.

Fake fur kept the water warm longest. My data supported my hypothesis.

Go further.

Use what you learn. Think of new questions to test or better ways to do a test.

Ask a Question

State Your Hypothesis

Identify and Control Variables

Test Your Hypothesis

Collect and Record Your Data

Interpret Your Data

State Your Conclusion

Go Further

Science Tools

Scientists use many different kinds of tools. Tools can make objects appear larger. They can help you measure volume, temperature, length distance, and mass. Tools can help you figure out amounts and analyze your data. Tools can also help you find the latest scientific information.

You should use **safety goggles** to protect your eyes.

You use a **thermometer** to measure temperature. Many thermometers have both Fahrenheit and Celsius scales. Scientists usually use only the Celsius scale.

You can use a **telescope** to help you see things that are very far away, such as stars and planets.

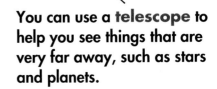

Binoculars make far-away objects appear larger, so you can see more of their details.

A **hand lens** doesn't enlarge things as much as a microscope does, but it is easier to carry.

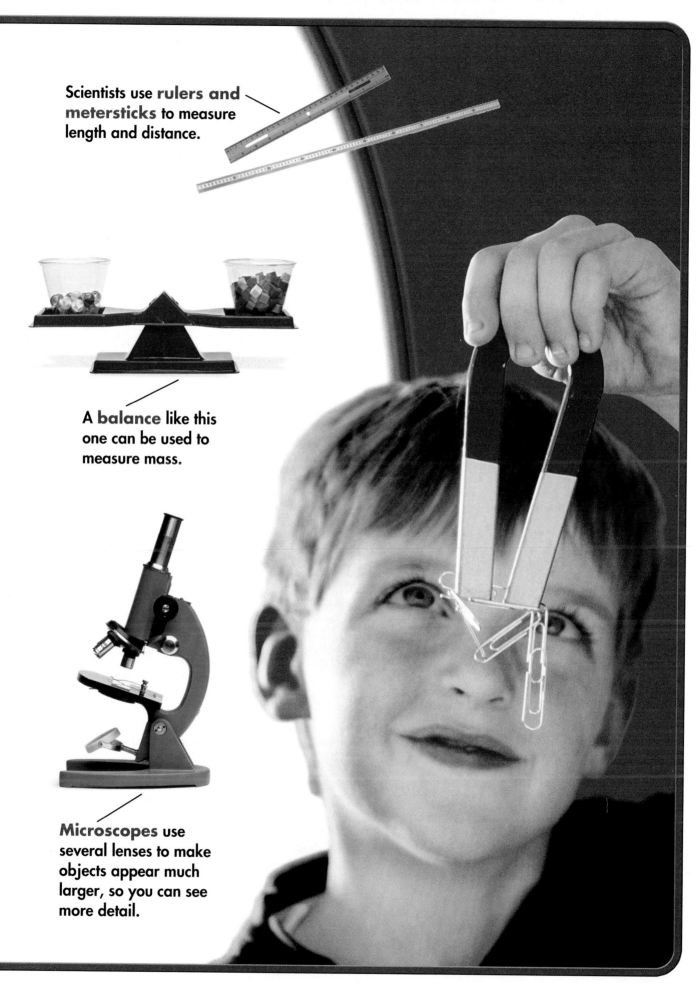

Scientists use **rulers and metersticks** to measure length and distance.

A **balance** like this one can be used to measure mass.

Microscopes use several lenses to make objects appear much larger, so you can see more detail.

Science Tools

Magnets can be used to test if an object is made of certain metals such as iron.

Pictures taken with a **camera** record what something looks like. You can compare pictures of the same object to show how the object might have changed.

A **graduated cylinder** can be used to measure volume, or the amount of space an object takes up.

Calipers can be used to measure the width of an object.

You can figure amounts using a **calculator**.

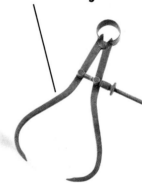

Scientists use **computers** in many ways, such as collecting, recording, and analyzing data.

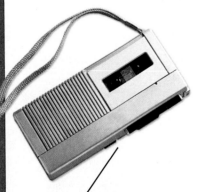

You can talk into a **sound recorder** to record information you want to remember.

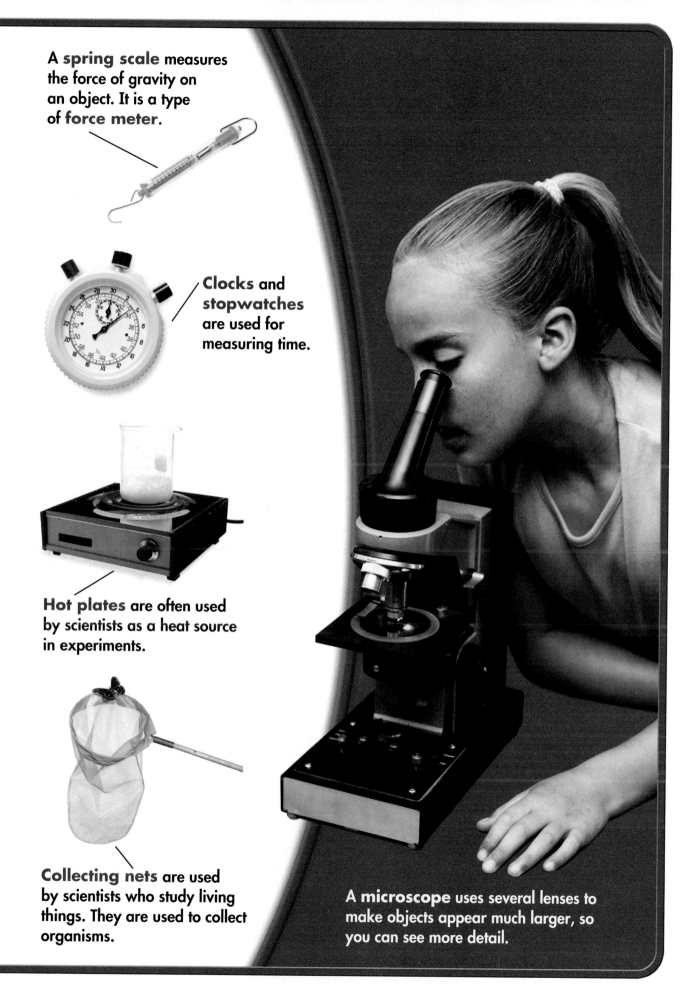

A **spring scale** measures the force of gravity on an object. It is a type of **force meter**.

Clocks and **stopwatches** are used for measuring time.

Hot plates are often used by scientists as a heat source in experiments.

Collecting nets are used by scientists who study living things. They are used to collect organisms.

A **microscope** uses several lenses to make objects appear much larger, so you can see more detail.

Safety in Science

You need to be careful when doing science activities. This page includes safety tips to remember:

- Listen to your teacher's instructions.

- Read each activity carefully.

- Never taste or smell materials unless your teacher tells you to.

- Wear safety goggles when needed.

- Handle scissors and other equipment carefully.

- Keep your work place neat and clean.

- Clean up spills immediately.

- Tell your teacher immediately about accidents or if you see something that looks unsafe.

- Wash your hands well after every activity.

- Return all materials to their proper places.

Chapter 10
Matter and Its Properties

You Will Discover

- how to observe and describe matter.
- the different states of matter.
- ways to measure different properties of matter.

online
Student Edition
sfsuccessnet.com

Discovery Channel School
Student DVD

What are the properties of matter?

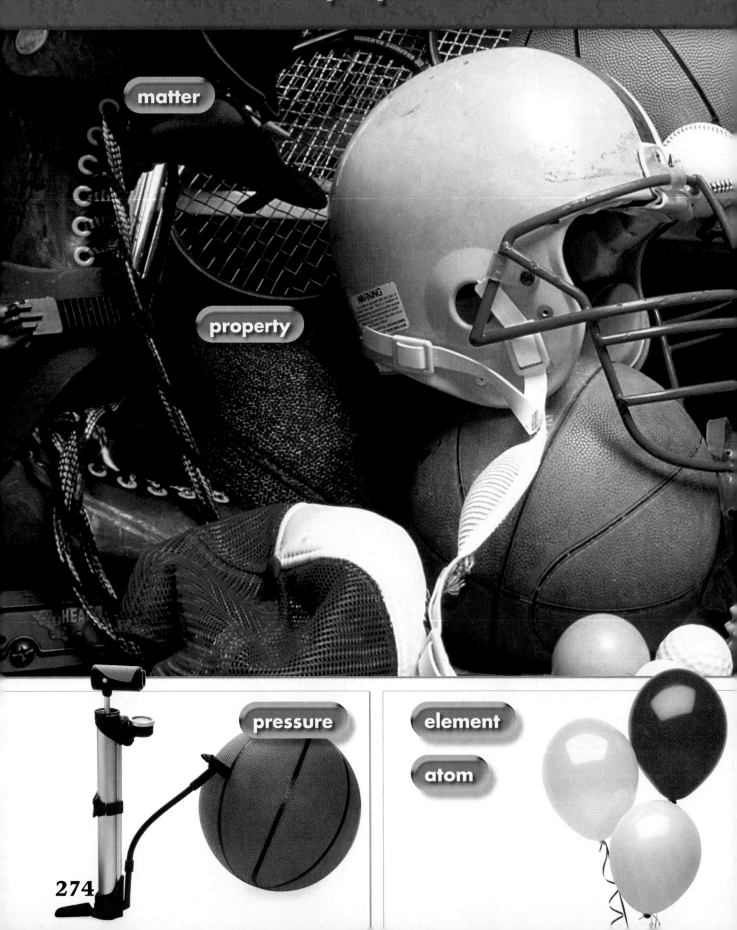

matter

property

pressure

element

atom

274

Chapter 10 Vocabulary

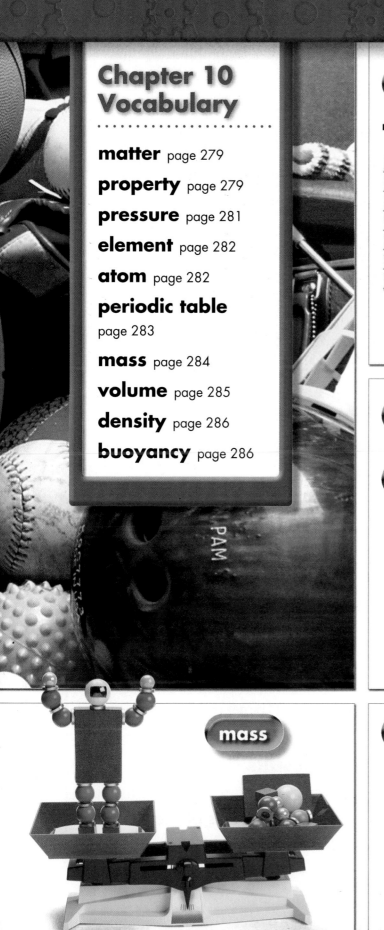

periodic table

Periodic Table of Elements

State at Room Temperature
= Solid   = Liquid   = Gas

density

buoyancy

mass

volume

Explore Which material has a surprising property?

Materials

safety goggles

resealable plastic bag

water

tub

3 sharpened pencils

What to Do

Seal bag!

half full

Hold over tub!

1 Put water in the plastic bag.

What do you think would happen if you push a pencil into the bag?

2 Slowly push a pencil into the bag. **Observe**. Based on your observations, **infer** why the result occurred.

Discuss the results with other students. Think about their explanations.

3 Based on your observations, **predict** what will happen if you push the pencil point out the other side. Try it.

Push 2 more pencils into the bag. See if you get the same results.

Process Skills

When you made your **prediction**, you used what you had just **observed** to help **infer** what would happen.

Explain Your Results

Compare your **prediction** in step 3 with your **observation**. Draw diagrams or sketches to show your prediction and your result.

How to Read Science

Cause and Effect

- A **cause** makes something change. An **effect** is the change you **observe**. Sometimes science writers use clue words and phrases such as *because, so, since,* and *as a result* to signal cause and effect.

- With careful **observations**, you might **predict** an effect that a certain cause will have.

Science Article

The Matter with Juice

Justin poured some juice from a bottle into a glass. Because juice is a liquid, its shape changed when it was in the glass. He decided to measure how much juice he had, so he poured it into a measuring cup. Then he decided to make a solid, so he put the juice into a mold and put sticks in it. He put the mold in the freezer. As a result, he had a frozen juice bar!

Apply It!

Make a graphic organizer like the one shown. Then use it to list two **causes** and two **effects** from the science article.

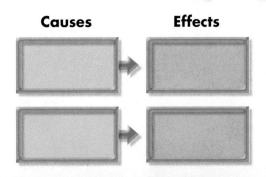

Causes   **Effects**

You Are There!

You walk into a room and see all these objects. Wow! It's a sports-lover's dream! You look around for the item you need for your favorite game. How do you find it among all of this stuff? Well, you look for certain colors, sizes, and shapes. Let's see now . . . Ah! There it is. What makes it different from all the rest?

AudioText

Lesson 1

How can we describe matter?

Everything you can see, smell, or touch is matter. Many things that you cannot see, smell, or touch are matter too.

A World of Matter

All of the objects you see around you are made of matter. **Matter** is anything that takes up space and has mass. You can feel the mass of objects as weight when you pick them up. When you blow up a balloon, you see that even air takes up space.

A **property** is something about matter that you can observe with one or more of your senses. A ball looks round and feels smooth or bumpy. It could be hard or soft. The sound of it bouncing off the floor tells you more about the ball's properties. For other kinds of matter, such as a flower, your sense of smell tells you about other properties.

These balls, the hockey puck, the baseball mitt, and the air inside the tennis ball are matter.

1. **✓Checkpoint** What is *matter*?

2. **Writing in Science** **Expository** Draw two columns titled *Object* and *Properties*. Fill in the box with the properties of some things you see. Choose one object and write a paragraph using the information in the Properties column. Exchange your paragraph with a classmate. Try to guess each other's object.

States of Matter

All the matter around you is a solid, a liquid, or a gas. Each kind of matter is made of very small particles. These particles are so small that you cannot see them, even under a magnifying lens. The particles always move. In some kinds of matter they just jiggle. In other kinds they slide past one another or bounce around.

Solids

The bowling ball is a solid. You can put it over a small opening to a large container. But the ball won't change shape and fall through the opening. Like other solids, the ball keeps its shape. The particles of a bowling ball, or any other solid, are held tightly together. They jiggle or vibrate very fast. However, they stay firmly in place.

Liquids

Look at the orange juice being poured into a glass. The juice is a liquid. It will take the shape of the glass into which it is being poured. The particles of orange juice, or any other liquid, are loosely held together. The particles can flow past one another. If you pour the orange juice from the glass into another container, the juice will change shape again. However, the juice will take up the same amount of space in the new container.

Orange juice is a liquid. The particles of juice are loosely held together.

A bowling ball is a solid. The particles of the ball are firmly held together.

Gases

The air being pumped into the basketball is a gas. When you pump air into a ball, the air fills the space. Like other gases, air has no shape. The tiny gas particles are not held together. They bounce off one another as they move freely. Unlike solids and liquids, the amount of space that air takes up changes. The air spreads out, or expands, to fill whatever space is available.

As air is pumped into a ball, the air at first expands. It starts to push against the inside of the ball. This pushing is called **pressure**. As the ball is filled, the air becomes more compact. It presses together. You can feel the pressure by pushing on the ball before and after air is added.

1. ✔**Checkpoint** What are three states of matter?

2. **Cause and Effect** How does melting ice into water, and then letting the water evaporate, change the state of the ice?

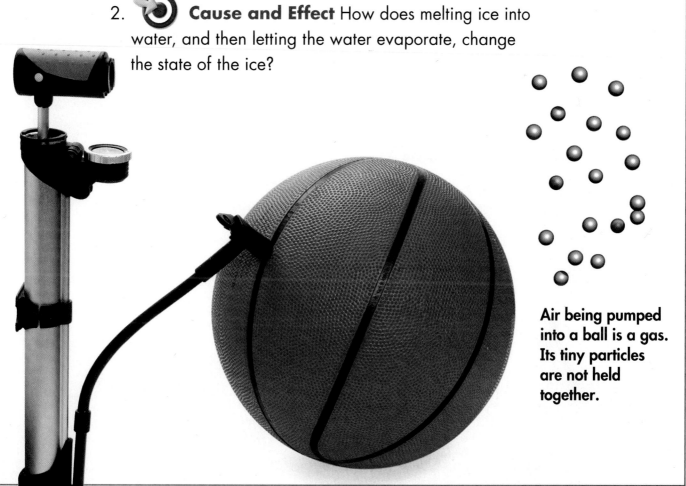

Air being pumped into a ball is a gas. Its tiny particles are not held together.

Parts of Matter

Suppose you could break a chunk of gold into smaller and smaller pieces. Each piece of gold is still the matter we call gold. Gold is an element. An **element** is matter made of a single type of particle too small to see. A chunk of gold is made only of particles of gold.

Most matter, however, is made out of many types of particles combined together in different ways. The smallest particle of an element that has the properties of that element is an **atom.** Gold is made up of atoms of gold. Clay, however, is made up of different kinds of atoms. These atoms act together to give clay its properties.

A particle of clay is made of different kinds of atoms. The atoms act together to give clay its properties.

The helium that fills these balloons is an element.

Clay pots are made of particles of clay.

Science experiments show that there are more than 100 different elements. Scientists arrange these elements in a **periodic table** of the elements. Elements are arranged based on their properties. Examples include how they respond to heat and other elements. This table is shown below.

Empedocles

Empedocles [em PED uh KLEEZ] lived in ancient Greece. He and others thought that earth, air, fire, and water were the four elements that made up all matter.

Periodic Table of Elements

State at Room Temperature
= Solid   = Liquid   = Gas

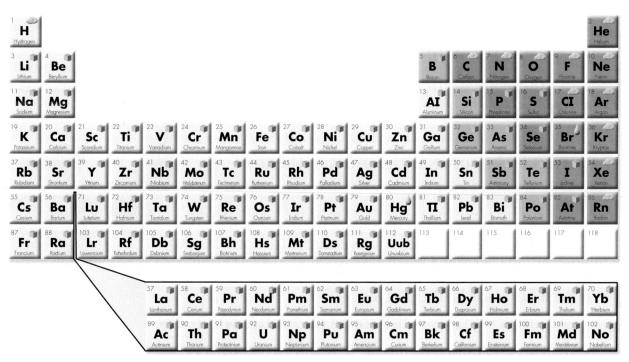

In the periodic table, elements in the same column have similar properties.

✓ Lesson Checkpoint

1. Explain why most objects you observe are not elements.

2. What about elements is used to arrange them in the periodic table of the elements?

3. **Social Studies** in Science Use library resources to find out about atoms. Find out who first used the word *atom*.

Lesson 2

How are properties of matter measured?

You can observe many properties of matter through your senses. You also can use tools to measure some properties of matter.

Tools for Measuring Mass

One property of matter that you can measure is mass. An object's **mass** is the amount of matter it has. Solids, liquids, and gases all have mass. One tool used to measure mass is a balance. The two pans shown are at the same level. They are in balance. The mass of the toy on the left is the same as the mass of the toy's pieces on the right.

A metric unit for mass is the gram (g). Larger amounts of matter are measured in kilograms (kg). There are 1,000 grams in a kilogram. The mass of a baseball bat is about 1 kg.

An object's mass is the same no matter where the object is. An object's weight is different in different places. Its weight is different on Earth, on the Moon, and in space. The scales in doctors' offices and grocery stores measure weight.

A balance measures mass or the amount of matter an object has. The whole toy has the same mass as its parts.

This table shows the mass of some common objects.

Mass of Common Objects	
paper clip	1 g
dime	2 g
pencil	5 g
mug	400 g
stapler	500 g

Tools for Measuring Volume

Another property of matter that you can measure is volume. An object's **volume** is the amount of space that the object takes up. Solids, liquids, and gases all have volume. To measure the volume of liquids, you use a cup with numbered units on its side or a graduated cylinder.

The basic metric unit for measuring the volume of a liquid is the liter (L). You will see numbers for parts of a liter on the side of the measuring cup. The smaller parts of a liter are milliliters (mL). There are 1,000 milliliters in a liter.

Solids have volume like liquids do. You can measure the volume of a solid using water. A solid, such as a small rock, will keep its shape in water. Fill a measuring cup with water half way. Record the water level. Place the rock into the water. Record the new level of the water. The difference in the water levels is equal to the volume of the rock.

The volume of the water in this measuring cup is 500 mL.

The volume of the milk in this jug is about 2 L.

The volume of the orange juice in this bottle is about 1 L.

The volume of the water in this water bottle is about 500 mL.

1. ✓**Checkpoint** How are an object's mass and weight different?

2. 🎯 **Cause and Effect** What effect would cutting a piece of wood in half have on the total mass of the wood?

285

Measuring Density

Density is another property of solids, liquids, and gases. **Density** is a measure of the amount of matter in a certain amount of space. A bowling ball is harder to lift compared to a rubber ball that is the same size. Both balls have the same volume. The bowling ball, however, has more mass. Therefore, the bowling ball has greater density.

You can study the density of matter in objects by observing how well they float in a liquid or a gas. This property of matter is **buoyancy.** Stones, for instance, have little buoyancy in water and they sink. Therefore, stones must have a higher density than water. Another example is a kind of salad dressing made of oil and vinegar. Oil is buoyant in vinegar, and it floats on top of vinegar. Vinegar is mostly water. Therefore, oil has a lower density than water. Balloons filled with helium are buoyant in air, and they rise. Therefore helium has a lower density than air.

This ball is the same size as the bowling ball. How could you tell which has more matter in it?

286

So far, we have looked at the density of objects compared to water or air. How do you compare the density of two solid objects with the same volume? To do this, you need to measure the mass and the volume of the two objects. Make sure the objects are equal in volume. Then the object that has the greater mass will be the one with greater density.

Knowing the density of matter helps scientists tell different kinds of matter apart.

Pennies

Marbles

Paper boat

Cork

These objects differ in their density compared to water. Predict which objects will sink and which will float.

An object will float in water if it has less density than water. It will sink if it has greater density than water.

1. ✓**Checkpoint** What is *density?*

2. **Writing in Science** **Expository** Write a paragraph in your **science journal** that explains how to tell which of two liquids has less density.

287

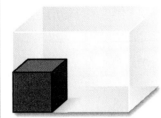

1 cubic unit

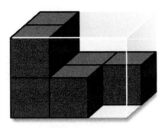

Fill the box with cubes to find its volume.

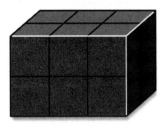

12 cubes fill the box. The volume is 12 cubic units.

Tools for Measuring Other Properties

Size is another property that can be measured. Length, for example, is the distance from one end of an object to the other end. Metric rulers and tapes are used to measure length. The basic metric unit of length is the meter. Shorter lengths are measured in centimeters (cm) or millimeters (mm). There are 100 cm in a meter. There are 1,000 mm in a meter. Much longer distances are measured in kilometers. There are 1,000 meters in a kilometer.

Other tools and units can be used to measure the volume of solid objects. A cubic unit is a cube that is used to measure volume. To find the volume of a box, you can find how many cubes of one size would fit inside the box. A cube that measures 1 centimeter on each side has a volume of 1 cubic centimeter. If 12 of these cubes fit inside a box and fill it up, the volume of the box is 12 cubic centimeters.

The tape measures the length of this model airplane's wingspan in centimeters. How long is the wingspan?

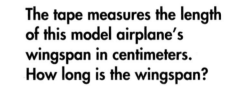

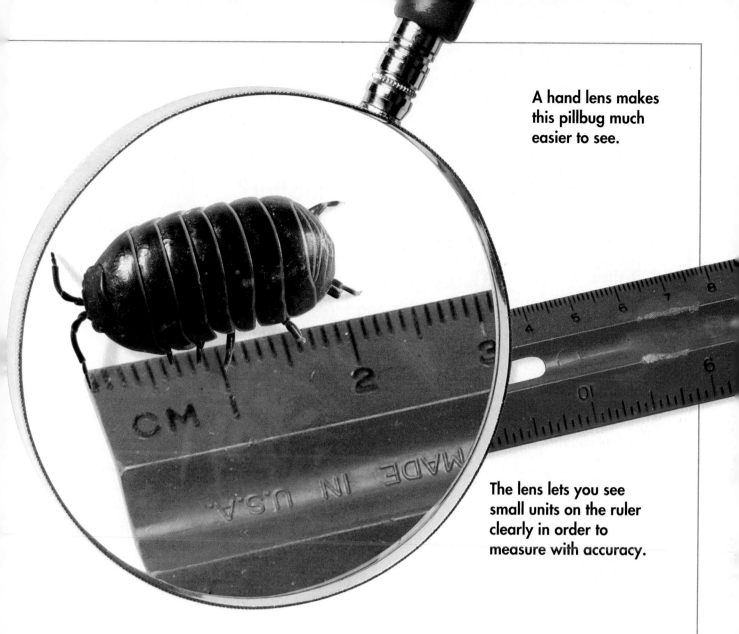

A hand lens makes this pillbug much easier to see.

The lens lets you see small units on the ruler clearly in order to measure with accuracy.

Some objects are too small to see easily. For instance, you may need a hand lens or magnifying glass to observe and measure the properties of a pillbug. If you put a metric ruler under the lens, you can more easily measure the length of the pillbug.

✓ Lesson Checkpoint

1. Describe how you would measure the volume of a liquid.

2. How could you measure the volume of a box?

3. **Math** in Science   What is the basic metric unit for length? What units are used to measure shorter lengths?

Investigate How can you measure some physical properties of matter?

Materials

sponge and small notepad

wooden block, small box, dot cube

metric ruler

balance and gram cubes

What to Do

1 Use the ruler to **measure** the length of the notepad. Measure to the nearest centimeter. Record the length.

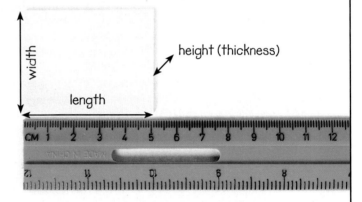

2 Follow the directions in step 1 to find the width of the notepad. Then find its height.

3 Measure the mass of the notepad. Balance the note pad with gram cubes. Record the mass.

Process Skills

Sometimes **measurements** can be slightly different, even though what is being measured stays the same.

4 Repeat steps 1 to 3 to find the measurements of the wooden block, small box, number cube, and sponge.

5 Compare your measurements with those of other groups. Repeat your measurements.

Object	Length (cm)	Width (cm)	Height (cm)	Mass (g)
			7.7 cm	
			10 cm	
			10.9 cm	
			1.5 cm	

Explain Your Results

1. **Interpret Data** Which object has the most mass? Which has the least mass?

2. Were your **measurements** the same as those of other groups? When you repeated your measurements, were they the same? Why do you think measurements might be different?

Go Further

How can you measure larger objects? What units can you use for measuring? Can you invent a new way to measure? Choose a question and make a plan to answer it.

Measuring Properties

Different tools and different units are used to measure volume, length, and mass.

The volume of liquid in the measuring cup is 90 milliliters. The graduated cylinder has the same amount of liquid in it.

The small marks on the ruler mark off millimeters. There are 10 mm in 1 cm, so you can count by tens to find the length in millimeters. The paper clip is 30 mm long.

Eraser

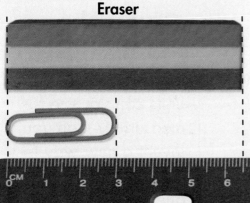

The paper clip is 3 centimeters long.

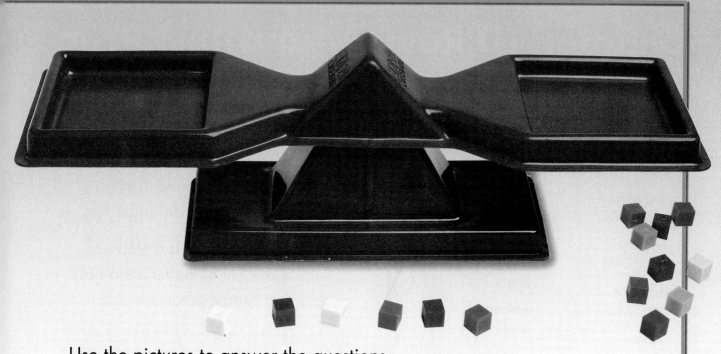

Use the pictures to answer the questions.

1 The eraser is more than 6 cm but less than 7 cm long. What is its length in millimeters?

A. 6 mm
B. 65 mm
C. 650 mm
D. 6000 mm

2 Which tool would you use to find the mass of a marble?

F. graduated cylinder
G. metric ruler
H. pan balance
I. measuring cup

3 Which has the greatest volume?

A. 1 liter of milk
B. 500 milliliters of milk
C. 50 milliliters of milk
D. 5 milliliters of milk

Lab zone Take-Home Activity

Use a metric measuring cup and a metric ruler to measure properties of liquids and objects around your home. Compare the volumes of liquids and the lengths of objects.

Use Vocabulary

atom (page 282)	**periodic table** (page 283)
buoyancy (page 286)	**pressure** (page 281)
density (page 286)	**property** (page 279)
element (page 282)	**volume** (page 285)
mass (page 284)	
matter (page 279)	

Use the vocabulary word from the list above that best completes each sentence.

1. An object's _____ is the amount of matter it has.

2. When you see that a ball is red, you are observing a(n) _____ of the ball.

3. Each of the tiny particles that make up an element is called a(n) _____ .

4. A measuring cup is used to find a liquid's _____.

5. A balloon gets larger when air is blown into it because of air _____.

6. An object that floats in water has _____ in water.

7. Anything that takes up space and has weight is _____.

8. Elements are arranged in a(n) _____ based on their properties.

9. An object's _____ is a measure of the amount of matter the object has in a certain amount of space.

10. Matter that has only one kind of atom is a(n) _____.

Explain Concepts

11. List the two properties of matter that are needed to measure density and explain why you need to measure both.

12. List the following metric units from the smallest to the largest: meter, millimeter, kilometer, centimeter.

Process Skills

13. **Predict** You pour juice from a tall, narrow glass into a short, wide glass. What happens to the volume of the juice?

14. **Infer** An object falls into a pond and sinks. What do you know about the density of the object?

☉ Cause and Effect

15. Carrie and her friends wanted to play soccer. Their ball was too soft, so they needed to use a pump. Explain how the pump changed the ball so they could play with it. Use a graphic organizer to show all the causes and their effects.

Causes	Effects

Test Prep

Choose the letter that best completes the statement or answers the question.

16. How many states of matter can we observe?

(A) 1   (B) 2
(C) 3   (D) 5

17. Which tool is used to observe the visible properties of a tiny object?

(F) balance
(G) metric ruler
(H) graduated cylinder
(I) hand lens

18. If you weigh an object and then break it into two pieces, the sum of the weights of its pieces will be

(A) less than the weight of the object.
(B) equal to the weight of the object.
(C) greater than the weight of the object.
(D) half the weight of the object.

19. About how many different elements are there?

(F) 3   (G) 5
(H) 100   (I) 500

20. Writing in Science

Expository Make a chart that shows what tools and metric units are used for measuring mass, volume, and length.

Measurement	Tool	Unit
mass		
volume		
length		

Write a paragraph that tells what the chart shows.

Chemist

Do you like to cook? When you cook you use chemistry. Chemistry is the study of substances and how they change. You might not want to eat all the ingredients separately. After they are mixed and baked, however, they change. Then they taste just right.

Chemists also study the properties of substances. Some materials mix together easily. Sugar dissolves in water quickly. Other substances do not mix together well. Dr. John Pojman is a chemist. He directs experiments that are done in space where gravity won't interfere.

Dr. Pojman and other scientists are developing experiments to find out more about the ways that liquids mix together.

Chemists earn a degree in chemistry. Then they work for companies that make food, plastics, and medicine. Many chemists work for NASA.

Dr. John Pojman does experiments with fluids in low-gravity conditions.

Lab zone Take-Home Activity

Plastics are made from different substances. Each type of plastic has different properties. Find objects around your home that are made of plastic and list their properties.

EC NTL 10 9 8 7 6 5 4 3

Chapter 11
Changes in Matter

You Will Discover

- how physical changes affect matter.
- different ways to mix materials together.
- how we use chemical changes every day.

online
Student Edition
sfsuccessnet.com

Discovery Channel School
Student DVD
Discovery CHANNEL SCHOOL

What are physical and chemical changes in matter?

physical change

mixture

solution

298

Chapter 11
Vocabulary

chemical change

states of matter

Explore How can matter change?

Materials

safety goggles

3 cups

ice cube

spoon

water, vinegar, graduated cylinder

salt and baking soda

masking tape

What to Do

1 Put 100 mL of water and 1 spoonful of salt in cup A. Stir.

2 Put an ice cube in cup B.

3 Pour 50 mL of vinegar in cup C. Add 1 spoonful of baking soda. **Observe** the contents of each cup right away and after 10 minutes.

Be careful!
Wear safety goggles!

Label the cups A, B, and C.

100 mL water, 1 spoonful salt

1 ice cube

50 mL vinegar, 1 spoonful baking soda

Process Skills

Using knowledge obtained by reading the activity and **observations** made during the activity, you were able to make an **inference**.

Explain Your Results

Infer Think about the changes you **observed**. In which cup do you think a different kind of matter formed?

How to Read Science

TARGET SKILL

Cause and Effect

- A **cause** makes something change. An **effect** is a change you **observe.** Science writers use clue words and phrases such as *because, so, since,* and *as a result* to signal cause and effect.

- A cause may have more than one effect. An effect may have more than one cause.

Science Article

Chemical Properties and Changes

Nothing shines quite like a bright new penny. But over the years, the copper on the outside of the penny changes. It becomes dull brown. Then it becomes dull light green. The copper changes into a new kind of matter. That's a chemical change. The new matter forms because copper reacts with air. The ability to react with air is a chemical property of copper.

Apply It!

Make a graphic organizer like the one shown below. Fill it in to show the **inferred cause** and each **effect** from the article.

Cause	Effect

🔊 You Are There!

You stand at the base of the great mountain. The noise of heavy equipment fills your ears. Dust sticks in your nose and throat. You look up at the top of the mountain— and can hardly believe your eyes! A huge face of stone stares out over the distant land. Amazing! What kinds of changes are happening to that mountain?

🔊 AudioText ◀))

Lesson 1

What are physical changes in matter?

Physical properties such as size, weight, color, and position can change. Materials can also change state.

Making a Physical Change

The people in the picture are carving a statue of the Native American leader Crazy Horse out of this mountain. They are chiseling, hammering, and even blasting rock to bits. The bits of rock look different than the mountain. But each bit is still the same kind of rock as the whole mountain. The people are making a physical change to the mountain.

Matter goes through a **physical change** when it changes the way it looks without becoming a new kind of matter.

Cutting fruit into pieces causes a physical change. The pieces are made of the same kind of matter as the whole fruit.

1. ✔**Checkpoint** Describe a physical change in matter and explain why it is a physical change.

2. **Technology** in Science Use the Internet to find out more about the Crazy Horse Memorial project. Who started it? When did it begin? How long will it take to finish?

303

You make a physical change when you fold clothes.

Some Ways to Cause Physical Change

There are lots of ways to change how matter looks. The pictures show some of them.

One special type of physical change is a change in the state of matter. **States of matter** are the forms that matter can take—solid, liquid, and gas. Matter can change from one state of matter to another. Even if the state of one kind of matter changes, it remains the same kind of matter. For example, when liquid water freezes, it becomes ice, which is a solid. However, when ice melts, you can see that it is still water. Ice and water are the same kind of matter.

A change in the temperature of matter can cause it to change its state. For example, when water is heated to 100°C (212°F), it quickly evaporates. That means the water changes from a liquid into a gas. Even though you cannot see the gas, a physical change has happened. The water particles stay the same kind of matter. But the particles are so far apart that you cannot see them in the air. So even though the water has changed state, it has not become a new kind of matter.

As you know, water also changes its state when it is cooled. Above 0°C (32°F), the particles of liquid water slide past one another. At 0°C, water changes from a liquid to solid ice. Each water particle slows down and vibrates very fast in place.

When you cut paper you are making a physical change.

And what happens when you hold an ice cube in your fist? The heat from your hand makes the water particles move faster. They no longer vibrate in place. They move freely, flowing as liquid water, which you feel dripping through your fingers. But no matter how many physical changes you make, the amount and kind of matter remain the same.

You can make a sculpture of water only when it's in a solid state.

In ice, water particles vibrate in place.

In liquid water, the water particles slide past one another.

Some water has evaporated. The water particles in the gas called water vapor are far apart.

States of Water

✓ Lesson Checkpoint

1. List ways that you can make physical changes in matter.

2. What physical changes happen to water as it freezes?

3. **Cause and Effect** Make a graphic organizer like the one on page 301. Fill it with ways to cause physical changes to a piece of paper. Describe the effects each change would have on the paper.

305

Lesson 2

What are some ways to combine matter?

The different coins in this mixture can easily be separated.

Many kinds of matter can be combined. Sometimes you can separate substances from the combination.

Mixtures

Each single coin on this page is made up of matter. So what happens when you put all these different pieces of matter together? You get a mixture. A **mixture** is made of two or more kinds of matter that are placed together. The amounts of each kind of matter do not have to be the same. For example, there may be more quarters than pennies in the coin mixture. But it's still a mixture. In fact, each coin is a mixture. Two or more metals are melted together to form each type of coin.

What parts make up this mixture?

What is important about a mixture is that each kind of matter in it does not change into another substance. Each kind of matter can also be separated from every other kind in the mixture.

Some mixtures are very easy to separate. For example, you can separate sand grains and marbles because of their size. You could put the mixture into a strainer with fairly small holes. The marbles are too big to go through the holes of the strainer, but the sand pours right through.

You can also separate sand and iron pieces if you use a magnet. The magnet pulls the iron out of the mixture. The sand remains behind.

How does a magnet help separate the parts of this sand-iron mixture?

1. ✔ **Checkpoint** Give three reasons why a bowl of different kinds of beans is a mixture.

2. **Social Studies** in Science Find out what metals are melted together to make a penny, a nickel, a dime, and a quarter.

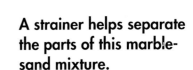

A strainer helps separate the parts of this marble-sand mixture.

Has this ever
happened to you?
Why does the gas
explode from the can?

Solutions

Have you ever mixed lemonade powder into water to make lemonade? After you stir the powder into the water, the powder seems to disappear. But it doesn't go away. It dissolves. This means the powder breaks into particles so tiny that you cannot see them. Also, the particles spread evenly throughout the water.

When one or more substances dissolve in another, a **solution** forms. A solution is a kind of mixture. Unlike the mixture of sand and marbles, though, you may not be able to see the particles in a solution. Even though you can't see the powder in the lemonade, you know it's there if you taste it.

You use all kinds of solutions. Soda is a solution of carbon dioxide gas and other substances dissolved in water. Shake a can of soda and the gas separates quickly from the water. In a closed can, the bubbling gas has no place to go. It builds up pressure. When you open the can, the gas escapes.

Straining doesn't separate the salt from salt water. But if you boil away the water, the salt is left behind.

Separating Parts of Solutions

Just like in other mixtures, you can separate the parts of a solution. Think about a pitcher of salt water. How can you separate the salt from the water after it's been mixed? You can try pouring the salt water through a strainer. That worked pretty well with the marble-sand mixture. But if you taste the water that runs through the strainer, it's still salty. The salt particles are too tiny to be trapped by the strainer.

What if you heat the salt water until it boils? The water evaporates. The salt is left in the container. You've done it! The salt separates from the water when the water evaporates. The same thing happens with lemonade. As the water evaporates, the substances in the powder stay behind.

Remember that all these "disappearing acts" are physical changes. The changes may make the substance look different. But each is still the same substance in the same amount.

Some substances, like lemonade mix, will dissolve in water.

Some substances, like these small stones, will not dissolve in water.

✓ Lesson Checkpoint

1. What makes ocean water a mixture?

2. What makes ocean water a solution?

3. **Writing in Science** **Descriptive** In your **science journal,** describe some things for a mixture. What do you think will happen when you mix them? Be sure to name the parts of your mixture.

309

What are chemical changes in matter?

Some changes in matter can produce new kinds of matter. We use these changes all the time.

Forming Different Materials

Mmmmm . . . there's nothing like the smell of fresh, warm bread. It tastes so good right out of the oven. But you wouldn't want to eat it before it was baked. A bowl of flour, baking powder, and eggs wouldn't taste very good.

In a **chemical change,** one kind of matter changes into a different kind of matter. A chemical change happens when bread is baked. The batter is a mixture of ingredients. But the heat of the oven causes chemical changes to happen. Then a new substance, bread, is formed.

A chemical change happens when eggs cook. They can never change back into the same form as raw eggs.

Baking bread produces a chemical change. You cannot get the ingredients back because a new substance is formed.

Remember that after water freezes into ice, the ice can melt back to water. Each change is a physical change. The water and ice are the same material. But what about the materials that make up the bread? Can you ever separate them from the bread? Probably not. Materials that have gone through a chemical change usually cannot be changed back to the original kind of matter.

Sometimes a chemical change can happen quickly. For example, fire can burn wood in minutes. Other times, a chemical change happens slowly. Think about an iron chain that's left outside. Aided by water, the iron slowly combines with oxygen gas from the air. Then the iron and oxygen change to rust. The rust is now a different kind of matter, and it will not change back into iron and oxygen gas.

Rusting is a slow chemical change.

Burning is a fast chemical change. When the sticks burn, the wood changes to gases and ashes. Some of the gases and ashes make up smoke.

1. ✔ **Checkpoint** How do you know that burning wood is a chemical change?

2. 🎯 **Cause and Effect** Let's say you paint an iron door the color of iron rust. Meanwhile, the bread you are baking turns a rust color on top. Which is a physical change? Which is a chemical change? Explain.

Using Chemical Changes

We use chemical changes every day. From eating pizza to watching a fireworks show, chemical changes are part of our lives.

Chemical changes start in your mouth the moment you begin to chew a piece of food. Then more changes happen as the food goes through your body. It's a good thing too. Chemical changes give your body the material it needs for energy and growth.

Chemical changes also help move us from place to place. Gasoline burning is a chemical change that releases the energy that the car's engine uses.

Chemical changes make many things in life easier to do. For example, laundry soap often has additives that cause chemical changes which break down stains. Without these changes, clothes might keep getting dirtier and dirtier.

Many soaps cause chemical changes that break down dirt and grime.

Burning gasoline in cars is a chemical change.

Chemical changes in batteries release electricity that appliances use.

You rely on the ability of many kinds of material to undergo chemical changes. When you turn the switch on your CD player, for example, chemicals will combine inside batteries. New substances will form. The chemical change will make a small amount of electricity to help you hear your favorite music.

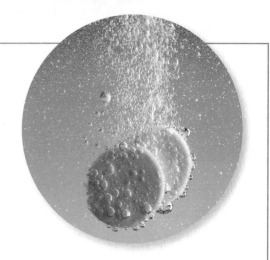

A chemical change between the water and the tablets causes the bubbles.

Chemical changes turn milk into cheese, like these large wheels of cheese at a factory.

✓ Lesson Checkpoint

1. What are four ways chemical changes are useful?

2. Does using a battery cause a physical change or a chemical change? Explain your answer.

3. **Health in Science** Many drugs cause chemical changes in the body. Why do you think it is important to take drugs only under a doctor's care?

313

Investigate How can properties help you separate a mixture?

In this activity you separate a mixture of particles using 2 physical properties—the size of the particles and their ability to dissolve in water.

Materials

safety goggles

spoon

4 foam cups

salt, sand, 3 marbles

warm water and graduated cylinder

pencil

coffee filter and rubber band

foil

Process Skills

You used what you knew about the physical properties of sugar and salt to make a **prediction**.

What to Do

1 Label the 4 cups *A*, *B*, *C*, and *D*. Put 1 spoonful of salt, 2 spoonfuls of sand, 3 marbles, and 100 mL of water in cup A. Stir the mixture for about 1 minute.

2 Make 4 holes in the bottom of cup B by pushing a pencil through the bottom of the cup from the inside.

3 Hold cup B over cup C. All at once, pour the mixture from cup A into cup B. Move cup B around to clean the marbles. Record the part of the mixture that was removed by straining.

Tap cup A as you pour. Less sand will stick in the cup.

Be careful!

Wear safety goggles!

4 Put a coffee filter in cup D. Fasten with a rubber band. Slowly pour the mixture from cup C into cup D. Record the part of the mixture that was removed by filtering.

5 Take off the filter. Dip the spoon in cup D. Let 2 drops of the liquid drip on a piece of foil. Let the liquid evaporate. Record the part of the mixture that was removed by evaporation.

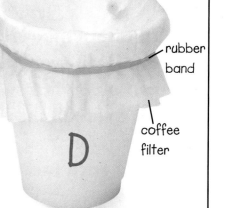

rubber band

coffee filter

D

You may need to leave the foil overnight.

Separating Method	Results of Separation	
	Part Removed	**Part Not Removed**
Straining		
Filtering		
Evaporation		

Explain Your Results

1. Which physical properties did you use to separate the mixture?

2. **Predict** Both sugar and salt dissolve in water. If you used sugar instead of salt, would your results change? Explain.

Go Further

How could you separate a mixture of iron filings, sand, and water? Make and carry out a plan to find out.

315

A Closer Look at Mixtures

Think about mixtures you have seen: a handful of sand and shells at the beach; a bowl of sweet, cold fruit salad; even all the stuff in your junk drawer. You can separate the parts of each mixture.

A can of mixed nuts contains the following:

15 cashews
6 pecans
12 walnuts
25 almonds
38 peanuts

This mixture is made of 5 different parts, or 5 kinds of nuts. All the nuts stay the same even when mixed. You can separate the nuts to learn more about the mixture. This mixture has a total of 96 nuts. Only 6 out of 96 nuts are pecans. There are fewer pecans than any other kind of nut. There are more peanuts than any other kind. Out of 96 nuts, 38 of them are peanuts.

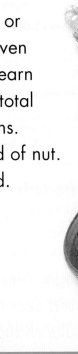

Listed below are parts of a mixture of cereal. The mass of each part is given.

35 grams of raisins

12 grams of almonds

133 grams of corn flakes

21 grams of dried cranberries

Use the information above to answer the questions.

1 What is the total mass of the cereal?

A. 220 grams   B. 212 grams

C. 200 grams   D. 201 grams

2 What is the order of parts in this mixture from greatest mass to least mass?

F. raisins, almonds, corn flakes, cranberries

G. cranberries, corn flakes, almonds, raisins

H. corn flakes, cranberries, almonds, raisins

I. corn flakes, raisins, cranberries, almonds

3 The amount of corn flakes is how much greater than that of all the other parts combined?

A. 65 grams   B. 54 grams

C. 100 grams   D. 133 grams

Lab zone Take-Home Activity

Find a mixture at home, such as rocks and shells like the ones shown. Separate the mixture into its parts. Make a chart listing the parts in order from greatest amount to least amount.

Use Vocabulary

chemical change (page 310)	**solution** (page 308)
mixture (page 306)	**states of matter** (page 304)
physical change (page 303)	

Use the vocabulary term from the list above that best completes each sentence.

1. A change in which the matter does not turn into a new kind of matter is called a _____.

2. Salt water is a _____ because one substance dissolves in another.

3. A _____ is two or more substances combined without changing any kind of matter.

4. A change in which one kind of matter is changed into another kind of matter is called a _____.

5. Solids, liquids, and gases are _____.

Explain Concepts

6. Explain why chopping wood is a physical change but burning wood is a chemical change.

7. Describe three different ways to cause a physical change.

Process Skills

8. **Infer** why a puddle of water can be on the sidewalk one day and be gone the next.

9. **Predict** what kind of a mixture you would have if you mix sugar and water.

10. **Predict** A dog dish of water is left outside during the night. The temperature will be −3°C during the night. What will happen to the water?

11. **Infer** Think of an egg frying in a pan. Does the frying produce a physical change or a chemical change? Give a reason for your answer.

12. **Draw Conclusions** When sugar is heated for a long time, it forms a solid black substance. What kind of change takes place? Explain your answer.

13. **Sequence** Put these steps in the correct order: ashes, paper, burning paper.

Cause and Effect

14. Make graphic organizers like the ones shown below. Fill in the correct cause and effect.

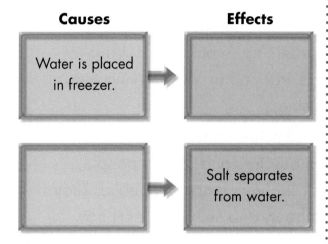

Causes   **Effects**

Water is placed in freezer. →

→ Salt separates from water.

Test Prep

Choose the letter that best completes the statement or answers the question.

15. Which of the following is a chemical change?

Ⓐ Water freezes.

Ⓑ Wire bends.

Ⓒ Paper is cut.

Ⓓ Wood burns.

16. A fruit salad is an example of a

Ⓕ change in state.

Ⓖ mixture.

Ⓗ solution.

Ⓘ chemical change.

17. What happens in a physical change?

Ⓐ The kind of matter remains the same.

Ⓑ The kind of matter changes to another kind.

Ⓒ Some of the matter changes to another kind.

Ⓓ The amount of matter changes.

18. In salt water

Ⓕ the parts become new kinds of matter.

Ⓖ the amount of each part is the same.

Ⓗ the parts cannot be separated.

Ⓘ the parts are mixed together in a solution.

19. Explain why the answer you chose for Question 18 is best. For each of the answers you did not choose, give a reason.

20. Writing in Science

Descriptive Write a paragraph describing what you see when you arrive at a forest fire. Include a description of chemical changes taking place.

Firefighter

This firefighter is teaching students about safety.

Each year fires kill people and destroy property. As a firefighter, you would work to prevent and control these disasters. You would drive and operate special trucks. You would assist in keeping them clean and in working order. You would learn ways to rescue people trapped in fires. Saving lives is serious business!

But not all of a firefighter's time is spent putting out fires and saving people. Sometimes firefighters teach the public. They might visit schools and show students how to be safe from fire at home. They also must train a lot and keep in good health.

You have to graduate from high school to become a firefighter. Then, if you can pass a physical and written test, you can go to firefighter training. Some firefighters go to college and study fire science. They learn a lot about how fires get started and how they spread.

Lab zone Take-Home Activity

On a piece of paper, design escape routes from each area of your house. Record the time it takes to move from each area through the proper exit.

Chapter 12
Forces and Motion

You Will Discover

- different ways to describe position and motion.
- how force affects motion.
- how simple machines work.

online
Student Edition
sfsuccessnet.com

How do forces cause motion and get work done?

position

motion

speed

relative position

gravity

322

Chapter 12 Vocabulary

force

friction

magnetism

work

323

Explore How can you describe motion?

Materials

2 balls

metric ruler

books or wooden blocks

2 long books

If you wish, you can use cardboard or wood to build your ramps.

What to Do

1 Make 2 ramps. Let go of a ball from the top of each ramp at the same time.

2 books

1 book

ball A

ball B

ramp A (higher ramp)

ramp B (lower ramp)

long books

2 **Observe** how each ball moves down the ramp. Does its speed increase or decrease? Which reaches the bottom first?

3 **Communicate** After each ball reaches the bottom, does its speed increase or decrease?

Explain Your Results

1. Which ball moved faster? Describe the location of each ball when it stops moving. Which was farther from the ramp?

2. **Communicate** Compare how a ball's speed changes before and after reaching the bottom of a ramp. Describe the 2 types of motion that you **observed**.

Process Skills

After the activity, you were able to **communicate** the 2 types of motion you **observed**.

How to Read Science

Summarize

When you **summarize** an article, you **communicate** all the information in just one or two sentences. Summarizing helps you remember what you read.

- Sometimes the summary is a sentence at the beginning or at the end of an article.

- Sometimes there is no written summary. Then you think about the pieces of information and summarize them.

Science Article

A World of Motion

Look around. Do you see anything moving? What about the second hand on the clock? Cars may be rolling by outside. Is anyone walking along the sidewalk? No doubt, we live in a world of motion.

Apply It!

Study the graphic organizer below.

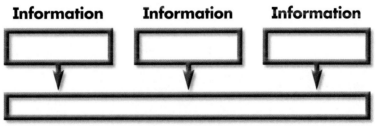

Make a graphic organizer like the one above. Write three details and the **summary** of the science article.

You Are There!

Here it comes—the wave you have been waiting for. You paddle quickly to get going. Then you stand up on your surfboard just as the monster wave arrives. Suddenly—whoosh! You're riding the wave. You're moving fast. The water crashes all around, but you keep your balance as you slice through the water. What a ride! Can you explain where you've been, where you've ended up, and how you got there?

AudioText

Lesson 1

What happens when things change position?

An object is in motion when its position changes. The speed and direction of an object's motion can also change. An object's position and motion depend on what you compare it with.

When Things Move

Can you tell when something is moving? Think about dropping a spinning top onto a hilly sidewalk. You can tell it has moved because its location has changed. It was in your hand. Now it's on the sidewalk spinning. If an object is in a different location, its **position** has changed.

A spinning top has circular motion. What else moves like a top?

Watch the top move down the sloping sidewalk in a certain direction. It is in **motion** as its position changes. It also moves in circles around a central point. The spin has given the top circular motion. You have made your top move down, then forward, and round and round as well.

1. **Checkpoint** How can you tell something is in motion?

2. **Writing** in Science **Descriptive** Write a paragraph in your **science journal** describing different kinds of motion you have observed.

327

Ways of Looking at an Object's Position

Have you ever gotten lost trying to get somewhere? Locating something can be confusing when you change position and everything else stays in place. For example, as you walk along, the water fountain is in front of you. After you pass by it, the water fountain is behind you. The fountain also seems to be moving away. The position, direction, and movement of an object often depend on how a person looks at it.

Sometimes a map might help locate things. A map is a drawing of a place. Those objects marked on a map are not real, of course. They are models of things. A map models the position of objects in relation to each other. Maps work because the objects on the map are fixed in place.

Suppose you have a map of a school like the one below. How would you describe a trip to the lunch room using position terms? You can use position words like *forward, left, right, behind,* as you move.

The arrows on the school map show a path from a classroom to the lunch room.

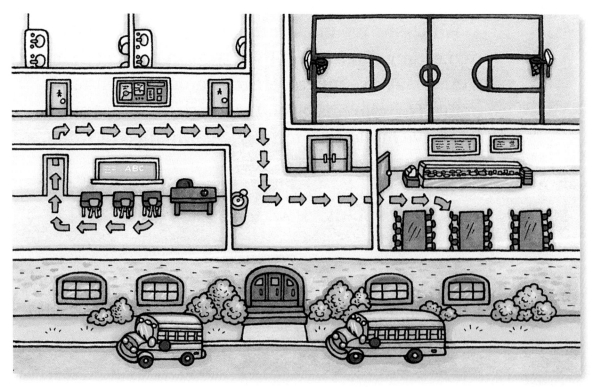

Positions of Moving Objects

The position of each object on a map is relative to other objects. *Relative* can mean that one thing depends on another thing for its meaning. When you tell about a trip to the lunch room, what you tell about would depend on your position.

What is the position of car 64 in the picture? You would say its relative position is in front of the other cars. **Relative position** is the position of one object compared with the position of other objects.

Is car 64 going to win? Only if its relative position when it crosses the finish line is in front of the other cars.

But what about cars that aren't in the picture? Some might be in front of car 64. You would say car 64 is behind the other cars. So the position of car 64 depends on the position of the other cars. The relative position of car 64 changes depending on the position of different cars.

Look at the train moving down the track. The locomotive is travelling in front of the two cars it is pulling. Could the cars move in front of the locomotive? They could if the train stopped and then started moving backward. The direction of their motion changes the relative position of objects.

When the locomotive is pulling the cars, it is in front of them. If it's pushing the cars, the locomotive is behind them.

1. ✓**Checkpoint** In what ways can the relative position of an object change?

2. **Social Studies** in Science
   Describe a trip to the lunch room of your school. Use position words.

How Fast Things Move

How fast does a jet plane fly? How fast does a caterpillar move? **Speed** is the rate, or how fast, an object changes its position. When things change position, they do so at a certain rate of speed.

Speed can be very fast. A jet plane moves fast. The two arms of the tuning fork are moving back and forth so fast they are just a blur. Did you ever see a meteor flash across the sky? It moves so fast that if you blink, you might miss it.

Speed can also be very slow. Some things have such a slow speed that you can't even see them move. The flowers in the picture have moved to face the light. If you turn the plant around, the flowers will slowly move back to face the light. The thick, syrupy honey is another slow mover. It moves slowly from the scoop down into the jar.

The arms of the tuning fork move back and forth very fast as they vibrate.

Constant Speed

Sometimes moving objects do not change how fast or slow they move. They are moving at a constant speed. Objects that move at a constant speed change position at the same rate. For example, suppose a car is moving steadily on a road at 35 miles an hour. It is moving at constant speed. Its speed, or rate, stays the same.

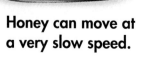

Honey can move at a very slow speed.

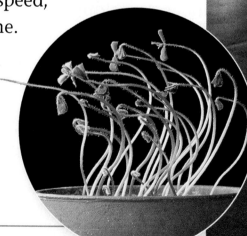

These flowers slowly change position as they grow toward the light. This motion is too slow to see.

Variable Speed

If you were in one of the bumper cars, you could change the direction of the car's motion. You could move forward, backward, to the side, or in a circle. You could also change the speed of the bumper car. You might try to bump into another car. You can cover the distance between you and the other car in less time by going faster. Maybe you can get away before the other car can bump into you!

The bumper cars move at a variable speed. Variable means that it changes. An object moving at a variable speed changes speed as it moves.

The bumper cars can move in different directions. They also can move at different speeds.

✓ Lesson Checkpoint

1. List at least three different ways objects can move.

2. What are four kinds of speed?

3. **Summarize** Write a sentence that summarizes what relative position is.

How does force affect motion?

Forces act on objects to change their motion. A force can involve two or more objects that contact each other. Other forces can act on an object without touching it.

The Causes of Motion

Did you push or pull a door open today? A **force** is any push or pull. A force can change an object's position or the direction of its motion.

Most of the forces you use are contact forces. When you push or pull an object, you must come in contact with, or touch, the object. When you hit a baseball with a bat, for example, the force of the bat changes the direction and the speed of the ball. If the bat doesn't make contact with the ball, these changes cannot occur.

How much an object changes its position and speed depends on how much force is used. If you push harder on a moving shopping cart, for instance, it will move faster. So, the greater is the force that acts on an object, the greater will be the change in its motion.

If the bat makes contact with enough force, the ball's change in speed and direction could take it out of the ballpark.

This shopping cart needs little force to start it moving, but wait until it's full!

Effects of Mass and Friction

How an object moves also depends on how much mass it has. When you start shopping in a grocery store, the cart is empty. You don't need to use much force to begin pushing it. As you fill it up with groceries, the cart gains more mass. Then you have to use more force to make it move.

While your grocery cart moves down the aisle, its wheels rub against the floor. This causes friction. **Friction** is a contact force that goes against the motion of an object. Friction can cause moving objects to slow down or stop.

The amount of friction between two objects depends on their surfaces. Pushing a grocery cart over smooth tiles in the store is pretty easy. You need more force to push the cart across the asphalt parking lot. The smooth tile produces less friction on the wheels than the asphalt does.

Sometimes friction is a helpful force. Think about a time you were skating or sledding and wanted to slow down or stop. What did you do? If you dragged your foot on the ground, the contact between your foot and the ground caused friction. The friction slowed you down.

1. ✓**Checkpoint** What is a force?

2. **Writing in Science**
   Narrative Make a two-column chart in your **science journal**. Head the first column, *Forces.* Head the second column, *Change.* Fill in the chart with different forces that you have used today. Include how the forces changed the position or speed of objects.

The greater mass of more carts causes you to use more force to get them going.

Motion and Combined Forces

You have learned that pushes, pulls, and friction change the motion of objects. Now, think about pulling on a rope in a game of tug-of-war. Your team's pull is a force in one direction. The pull of the other team is a force in the opposite direction. If the forces are equal, the rope does not move.

How can you win the game? If more join your team, you can pull with greater force. The pulls of everyone on your team combine with your pull to move the rope more easily in your direction. But what if even more join the other team? Their pulls combine to move the rope more easily in their direction. The rope will move in the direction of the stronger force.

The pulls of the two teams oppose each other. The team pulling with the greater force moves the rope in their direction.

The forces the cyclists are applying to their bikes overcome friction. These forces keep the bikes moving forward.

By shifting his weight, the rider can make the turn without losing speed.

Many forces cause a bicycle to change its motion. What are the forces when you ride your bike? Your legs push on the pedals. You shift your weight and push on one of the handlebars to turn. Friction between the bicycle's tires and the ground slows your forward motion. When you go uphill, you have to use more force. Going downhill, you may pick up too much speed. You pull on the handbrakes to slow down. All the time, wind pushes against you. You have to use forces all the time to keep moving forward. Each force has its own amount and acts in its own direction. All the forces must combine in order to keep the bicycle going forward safely.

What a workout!

The road produces less friction than the dirt path.

1. ✓**Checkpoint** What two things about forces are important when forces are combined?

2. **Math** in Science If two pulling forces applied to an object are in the same direction, would the forces be added together or subtracted?

335

Gravity and Magnetism

The forces you have learned about so far need objects to be touching or in contact. Another kind of force is a non-contact force. A non-contact force is a push or pull that can affect an object without touching it. **Gravity** is a non-contact force that pulls objects toward each other. These skydivers, for instance, are being pulled toward Earth by gravity. Without the force of gravity, they would all float away. Gravity pulls you and everything else on Earth toward Earth's center.

Gravity pulls the skydivers toward the ground.

Gravity pulls the bobsled down the hill. The sled speeds up quickly because the slippery ice surface causes little friction.

SciLinks Take It to the Net
sfsuccessnet.com
keyword: gravity
code: g3p336

The amount that gravity pulls on an object is its weight. An object's weight depends on where it is. Since the Moon has less gravity than Earth, for instance, you weigh less on the Moon. The pull of gravity is also less the farther you are from the center of Earth. So you weigh a little less on a mountaintop than you do at the base of the mountain.

The pull of gravity on an object depends on how much matter is in it. Objects with more matter have more mass. So the pull of gravity is greater if the object it is pulling has more mass. Even if the pull of gravity on an object changes, the object's mass remains the same.

Magnetism is another non-contact force. Magnets pull on, or attract, certain kinds of metal such as iron. For example, a strongly magnetic bar might pull a steel paper clip from halfway across your desk. Steel is a metal that has iron in it. Magnets do not attract wood, plastic, paper, or other objects that do not contain these metals.

A magnet does not affect a crayon because the crayon lacks metal that the magnet can attract.

✔ Lesson Checkpoint

1. What are three contact forces?

2. What are two non-contact forces?

3. **Math in Science** Denver, Colorado, is more than 1 kilometer above sea level. How would your weight in Denver compare to your weight on an ocean beach? How would your mass compare in both places?

Magnetism attracts these paperclips because they contain iron.

The soccer player applies force to change the direction of the soccer ball. Is work being done?

The snowball appears stuck, despite all the pushing. Is work being done?

How do simple machines affect work?

Work is done when a force moves an object. Simple machines help you do work more easily.

Work

Have you done any work today? In science *work* has a special meaning. You do **work** when you use a force and actually move an object. You do work when you move a shopping cart, rake leaves, or carry out the trash. But work can be fun too. You do work when you pedal your bike or kick a soccer ball down the field. The amount of work you do depends on how much force you use and how far you move the object.

Work is NOT done when the position of an object does not change. Imagine pushing against a big ball of snow with all the force you can. If the snowball does not move, no work is done. The football players are pushing against each other with as much force as they can. But the players are not moving in the direction they are pushing. No work is being done because none of the players have moved over a distance.

How much work can you do in one day? To answer this, you would need to add up the amount of pushing and pulling you do. You would then need to measure the distance those pushes and pulls moved things.

Suppose you put a library book back on its shelf. That would be a certain amount of work. How much more work would you do if you put the book on a shelf that is twice as high? The answer is twice as much work. What if you lift the book the same distance as the first time, but the book weighs twice as much? Again, the answer is you did twice as much work as you did the first time.

When Work Is Done	
Activity	**Work**
Thinking about a math problem	No
Turning a jump rope	Yes
Holding a puppy	No
Lifting a puppy	Yes
Pulling on a locked door	No
Opening an unlocked door	Yes
Trying to scoop rock-hard ice cream	No

Sometimes you do no work even when you make an effort to do so.

Football players collide and come to a stop. At this point, is work being done?

1. ✔ **Checkpoint** What is work?

2. **Writing in Science** **Expository**
In your **science journal**, write a paragraph that gives an example of work being done and work not being done. Explain why each example shows work or no work being done.

Instead of lifting the cart, the mover pushes the cart up a ramp.

The axe head is a wedge that separates the wood of the log.

Some Simple Machines

Making work easier is the reason for many inventions. Machines don't actually lessen the amount of work that is done. Machines help make work easier. Six kinds of simple machines help you do just that.

Inclined Plane

Look at the man pushing a cart up the ramp. Without the ramp, he would have to lift the cart straight up off the ground high enough to place it in the truck. That would take a great deal of effort. He is using a simple machine called an inclined plane. An inclined plane, or a ramp, is a slanting surface that connects a lower level to a higher level. The mover pushes the cart with less force over a longer distance. He still has the same amount of work to do, but it takes less effort to do it.

Wedge

Wedges are used to split, cut, or fasten things. A wedge is a simple machine made up of two slanted sides that end in a sharp edge. They act as a pair of inclined planes working together. When work is done with a wedge, the wedge moves through the material being worked on. The material separates as it slides up the sides of the wedge. A knife cutting through a pie, and a nail moving through a piece of wood are wedges.

A screw is an inclined plane wrapped around a center post.

This slide is an inclined plane wrapped around a center post. It is a kind of screw!

Screw

A screw is an inclined plane wrapped around a center post. A good example of how a screw looks is the spiral slide in the picture. Do you see how the slide wraps around the center post?

The slide is similar to a screw you use with a screwdriver. Screws can be used to hold things together, and to raise and lower things. When you open a jar, the lid raises if you turn it one way and lowers if you turn it the other way. The jar lid is a screw.

Lever

A seesaw is an example of a simple machine known as a lever. A lever is a stiff bar that rests on a support. A lever is used to lift and move things. If you push down on one side of the bar, you can raise an object on the other side.

A seesaw is a lever that rests on a support.

1. ✔**Checkpoint** What is an inclined plane?

2. 🎯 **Summarize** State briefly how using an inclined plane makes work easier.

support

341

More Simple Machines

Wheel and Axle

When you turn a doorknob to open a door, you are using a simple machine called a wheel and axle. The knob is a wheel and the post that attaches to its center is an axle. You would use less force to turn the doorknob a far distance than to turn the axle attached to the knob a shorter distance. This makes opening the door easier, although the work is the same.

A Ferris wheel and merry-go-round use a huge wheel and axle too. Instead of turning the wheel, however, the motor in these rides turns the axle. The distance over which the motor turns the axle is small. But the distance the axle turns the wheel is great. The force applied to the axle to do this must be great. The people on the ride are having fun. They probably are not thinking about the simple machine at work.

What kind of simple machine are the Ferris wheel and merry-go-round?

Pulley

Sailors pull sails to where the sails can fill with wind and push the sailing ship. But the sailors have to move the sails in directions that are uncomfortable for them. Simple machines called pulleys can help them. A pulley changes the direction of motion of an object to which a force is applied. The sail is attached to a pulley. The pulley has a grooved wheel that turns on an axle. The sailors can pull on the rope to turn the grooved wheel. As they pull the rope toward them, the sail is pulled in the proper direction. Now they are ready to hit the high seas!

Pulleys, like those on the boat above, help workers reposition heavy sails.

✓ Lesson Checkpoint

1. How do you know when a simple machine has done work?

2. What simple machine has a grooved wheel, an axle, and a rope?

3. **Summarize** Write a sentence that summarizes how simple machines are useful.

343

Investigate How much force will you use?

An overpass is an inclined plane.

Materials

string and paperback book

long book

2 books

meter ruler

spring scale

What to Do

1 Tie string around the paperback book.

2 Build an inclined plane. Use a ruler to measure its height.

3 Hook a spring scale under the string. Hold the spring scale and lift the book straight up to the height of the inclined plane.

Pull straight up.

The force of gravity pulls the book down. The scale measures the force you used to overcome gravity.

4 **Observe** the reading on the scale. Record.

Process Skills

Before you **predict**, think about what you **observed** and about what you already know.

5 **Predict** what the scale will read when you pull the book up the inclined plane. Record.

6 Holding the scale, pull the book up the inclined plane. Observe the reading on the scale.

If you wish you can construct your ramp out of cardboard or wood.

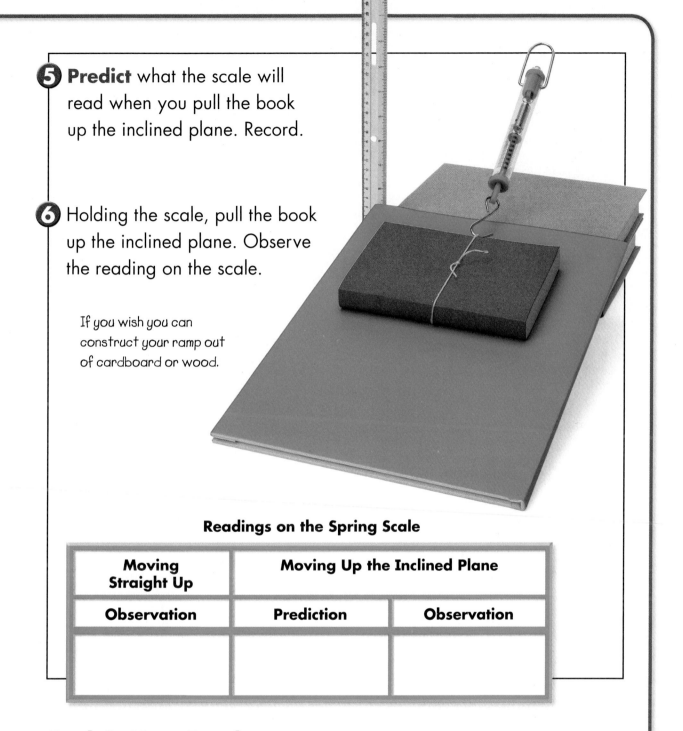

Readings on the Spring Scale

Moving Straight Up	Moving Up the Inclined Plane	
Observation	Prediction	Observation

Explain Your Results

1. What information did you use to make your **prediction**?

2. Compare your **observations**.

3. **Infer** How do you think the steepness of the ramp affected the amount of force needed to pull the book up the ramp.

⌐ Go Further

Use your data to predict what would happen to the force if you changed the steepness of the ramp. Make a plan to test your prediction.

Relating Speed, Distance, and Time

In a race, the winner is the one who covers the total distance in the least amount of time. To win, you must have the highest average speed.

The following rules can help you find thedistance a racer moved, the length of time in motion, or the average speed while in motion.

$$\text{Distance} = \text{Time} \times \text{Speed}$$
$$\text{Time} = \text{Distance} \div \text{Speed}$$
$$\text{Speed} = \text{Distance} \div \text{Time}$$

This stopwatch can be started and stopped at any instant, and is thus useful for timing races.

For example, a runner could run 40 kilometers in 4 hours at an average speed of 10 kilometers per hour.

Distance	Time	Speed
$40 = 4 \times 10$	$4 = 40 \div 10$	$10 = 40 \div 4$

Use the rules on page 346 to answer each question.

1 How far could you run in 3 hours at an average speed of 12 kilometers per hour?

2 If you walked a half-marathon (about 21 kilometers) in 3 hours, what was your average walking speed?

3 How long would it take a race-walker to finish a marathon (about 42 kilometers) at an average speed of 7 kilometers per hour?

How can you find the avevage speed of this racer?

Lab zone **Take-Home Activity**

Plan a 2-hour trip to take with your friends, riding your bikes or walking. Choose a reasonable average speed and find out how far you could ride or walk each way, in order to be back home in 2 hours. Include time for rest stops.

Chapter 12 Review and Test Prep

Use Vocabulary

force (page 332)	**motion** (page 327)
friction (page 333)	**position** (page 327)
gravity (page 336)	**relative position** (page 329)
magnetism (page 337)	**speed** (page 330)
	work (page 338)

Use the vocabulary term from the list above that best matches each statement.

1. If an object is in a different location, it has changed _____.

2. An object is in _____ if its position is changing.

3. A force that slows down a moving object is _____.

4. A push or a pull is a _____.

5. How fast an object changes position is its _____.

6. A change in position of one object compared to another object is its _____.

7. The non-contact force of _____ pulls any two objects toward each other.

8. The non-contact force of _____ pulls objects that contain iron.

9. If you use force to move an object, you have done _____.

Explain Concepts

10. Explain how you can tell that an object is in motion.

11. A train is moving 435 kilometers (270 miles) per hour. A plane is flying 965 kilometers (600 miles) per hour. How much faster is the plane moving than the train?

12. Write a paragraph about a simple machine you have used and how it helped you do work.

Process Skills

13. **Infer** what would happen to a thrown baseball if gravity and air friction did not affect it.

14. **Predict** how much more work you would do lifting two identical books compared to lifting just one.

Summarize

15. Make a graphic organizer like the one below. Fill in the summary.

| Work is the force it takes to move an object a certain distance. | The amount of force it takes to move an object is called effort. | Machines change the amount of effort it takes to move an object. |

↓ ↓ ↓

 ## Test Prep

Choose the letter that best completes the statement or answers the question.

16. Friction is a
- (A) moving object.
- (B) contact force.
- (C) gravitational force.
- (D) magnetic force.

17. What machine is an inclined plane wrapped around a center post?
- (F) lever
- (G) pulley
- (H) wedge
- (I) screw

18. Which of the following describes a constant speed?
- (A) fast, slow, fast
- (B) slow, slower, slowest
- (C) fast, faster, fastest
- (D) fast, fast, fast

19. Explain why the answer you chose for Question 18 is best. For each of the answers you did not choose, give a reason why it is not the best choice.

20. **Writing in Science**
Descriptive Choose one of the skydivers on page 336 and describe the position of that person. Hint: You can use position words such as *to the left of, across from,* and *to the right of.*

Exercising in Space

Do you like to exercise? Running, playing ball, and bicycling are exercises that have motion, speed, and force. But you don't have to be moving to exercise your muscles. Pushing against a wall may not do any work, but the pushing force you use exercises your muscles.

On Earth, the force of gravity helps you exercise. That's because every time you lift your legs or arms, you have to lift them against the force of gravity. So, you have to give your arms and legs force, and that's good exercise. Suppose you are an astronaut aboard the Space Shuttle or the International Space Station. You do not feel the tug of gravity. The very high speed it takes to stay in orbit around the Earth is the reason. It reduces the effect of gravity to zero. You float around the cabin. This makes exercising in space harder than on Earth. Imagine trying to push against a wall on the shuttle. It just sends you off in another direction!

Astronauts have to wear weights on the treadmill used in space.

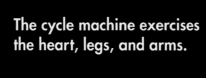

The cycle machine exercises the heart, legs, and arms.

Without exercise, your muscles and bones get weaker. Astronauts in space must exercise every day to keep their muscles and bones healthy.

Special exercise machines had to be built for space. One kind of machine is like an exercise bicycle. Another machine is like a treadmill. The third kind of machine is like a rowing machine that pushes and pulls on muscles. Astronauts have to be strapped to the machines so they don't float away. Then they put on weights so they can exercise their muscles.

Information learned about muscles and bones in space has helped people on Earth know more about keeping healthy. Many gyms on Earth have exercise machines based on those designed for space. This is just another example of how things developed for use in space can help us here on Earth.

Muscles and bones are made stronger by using the resistance machine.

Lab zone Take-Home Activity

On a piece of paper, design a machine, using pulleys and levers, that allows you to exercise one or more parts of your body.

The Wright Brothers

Orville and Wilbur Wright were inventors who changed the world. They had been making and selling bicycles. Stories of flying machines, however, got their attention.

The Wright brothers studied forces that affect the motion of aircraft. They knew about the forces that keep a craft in the air and pull the craft down. They also knew about the forces that move the craft forward and slow the craft's motion.

In 1902 they used their skills to build a successful glider. The Wright brothers became the first people to design, build, and fly a craft that could be successfully controlled by a pilot in the air.

Orville and Wilbur's next step was to design and build an aircraft that could fly using an engine. They had to build a gasoline engine that didn't weigh too much. Yet it had to provide enough force to move the craft in the air. In 1903, the brothers made the first controlled flight in an aircraft with an engine.

Lab zone Take-Home Activity

Ask each family member to design and build a paper plane. Have a contest to see which plane flies the farthest and the longest.

You Will Discover

- different forms of energy.
- how energy changes from one form to another.
- how energy travels.

Chapter 13
Energy

online
Student Edition
sfsuccessnet.com

How does energy change form?

reflect

kinetic energy

potential energy

absorb

354

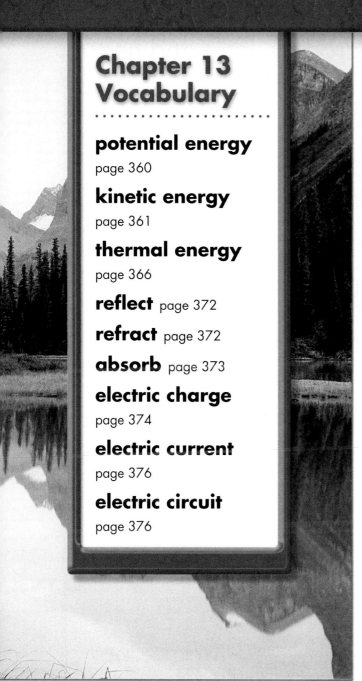

Chapter 13 Vocabulary

electric charge

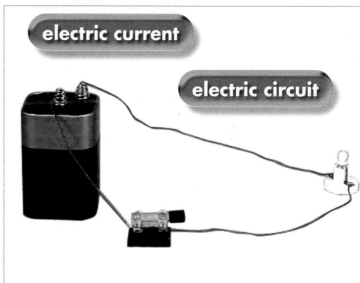

electric current

electric circuit

refract

thermal energy

355

Explore Can electricity produce light and heat?

Materials

safety goggles

2 pieces of wire

flashlight bulb and holder

battery and battery holder

thermometer

What to Do

Wear safety goggles. Be careful!

1 Make an electric circuit.

2 **Observe** the light.

The bulb of the thermometer should touch the light bulb.

3 Use a thermometer to observe heat. First, record the temperature you observe on the thermometer. Next, place the bulb of the thermometer against the light bulb for 1 minute. Then, record the temperature.

Explain Your Results

Explain the procedure. Name 2 forms of energy you **observed**. Describe where each was used or produced. Draw and label a diagram or sketch to help **communicate** your ideas.

Is every part of the circuit needed? Use your drawing to help predict, investigate, and describe what would happen if one part of your circuit were missing.

Process Skills

To help **communicate** clearly, scientists use sketches, diagrams, and drawings.

How to Read Science

Reading Skills

Main Idea and Details

- To find the topic of a paragraph, ask who or what the paragraph is about.

- To find the **main idea** in a paragraph, ask "What is the one important idea that all the sentences tell about?"

- To find supporting **details** in a paragraph, ask "Which sentences give information that supports the main idea?"

Science Article

Heating Homes

Energy heats your home. The energy comes from fuel that is burned. Some people heat their homes with natural gas. Some people burn wood to heat their homes. Other people use electricity. The electric company burns coal to make electricity. Gas, coal, and wood are natural resources. They come from Earth.

Apply It!

You can use a graphic organizer to **communicate** the **main idea and details.** Use one like this to show supporting details from the Science Article.

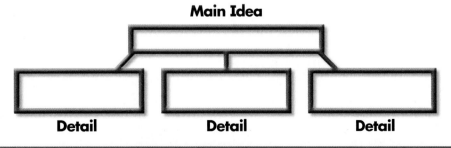

Main Idea

Detail   Detail   Detail

🔊 You Are There!

The Sun is shining brightly, but the air outside is cold. You stomp your feet and rub your hands together to warm them. You're looking forward to going inside and warming up. Maybe you'll listen to some music or play a DVD. How many different forms of energy will you use by the end of the day?

Lesson 1

What is energy?

The main source of energy on Earth is the Sun. Energy takes many forms. Energy can be stored and can change form.

Energy

Energy is the ability to do work or to cause change. Remember that work is done when a force makes an object move. You already know about the effects of the Sun's energy. Its warmth makes Earth a place in which we can live. The Sun's light energy makes plants grow. The Sun's energy also causes winds to blow and water to move through the water cycle.

How many things in this kitchen use energy?

We use many forms of energy in addition to the forms that come directly from the Sun. Electrical energy runs just about everything in this kitchen. Sound energy comes out of your CD player. Chemical energy in fuel runs the engine of a car. The energy of the car's motion gets you to the store. How do all these forms of energy come about?

1. **✓ Checkpoint** What are two forms of energy that Earth gets from the Sun?

2. **Writing in Science** **Descriptive** Write a paragraph in your **science journal** about the forms of energy you observe or use on your way to school.

Stored Energy

The skier uses energy that is stored in the body to ski across the snow. Stored energy is **potential energy.** It has the ability to change into another kind in order to do work or cause a change.

Fuels, such as oil, coal, natural gas, and gasoline, are other sources of potential energy. The energy stored in these fuels comes from sunlight. Long ago, plants used energy from sunlight to make food. After the plants died, they turned to a kind of fossil that we use as fuel. When we burn fuels, we release the potential energy within them to do work.

Every time you use batteries, you also release potential energy. The stored energy in food, fuels, and batteries is chemical energy.

Position or height stores another kind of potential enery. This energy is gained from gravity. The skier standing at the top of the hill has potential energy. So does a car at the top of a roller coaster and a playground swing at its highest point.

The standing skier has potential energy.

Gasoline contains the stored energy of living things that died long ago.

Batteries store energy as chemical energy.

360

Energy of Motion

Potential energy can change to kinetic energy. **Kinetic energy** is the energy of motion. When a car burns gasoline, for instance, potential energy stored in the gasoline changes to kinetic energy. The car moves. Look at the picture of the standing skier. When he pushes off, he goes down the hill. He's in motion. Potential energy stored in the skier's position at the top of the hill changes to kinetic energy. The force of gravity pulls him down the hill.

Many sources of energy are renewable. After a day of skiing, the skier can replace the energy he used by eating food. The skier can climb the hill again. You have learned that some sources of energy are not renewable. We cannot easily replace gasoline, natural gas, and other "fossil" fuels.

WHOOSH!

As the skier slides down the hill, potential energy changes to kinetic energy.

✔ Lesson Checkpoint

1. What are two kinds of potential energy?

2. Give two examples of potential energy and kinetic energy that you see every day.

3. **Main Idea and Details** Use a graphic organizer. What is the main idea of the paragraph at the top of this page? What details support it?

361

Lesson 2

How does energy change form?

Energy comes in different forms. Energy can change from one form to another. When energy changes form, some energy is given off as heat. People change energy into forms they can easily use, such as electricity.

Living things, such as this tarsier, change chemical energy stored in food to energy of motion and heat.

Changing Forms of Energy

Energy changes into more useful forms all the time. For example, your body stores potential energy as chemical energy. The chemical energy stored in your body changes to kinetic energy as you move.

Using Energy

You can't use the kinetic energy of your moving arm to make a light bulb burn bright. But you can use this kinetic energy to flip a light switch. This, in turn, helps change electrical energy to light energy. Most light bulbs also get hot. Some of the electrical energy changes to a kind of energy felt as heat. Energy cannot change completely from one form to another. Some energy is always given off in the form of heat.

Electrical energy changes to kinetic energy as the cable car moves along the track.

362

Forms of Energy

Chemical	Motion	Electrical	Light	Thermal

This energy holds the particles of matter together, such as in food. Eating food is the way we get energy.	This is the energy of moving objects. The moving parts in our machines and playground equipment have this form of energy.	This energy can pass through wires. This form of energy can change into forms that run appliances in our homes.	We see the Sun's energy in this form. Plants make food with light energy. We also change other forms of energy into light so we can see.	This form of energy makes particles of matter move faster. We feel this energy as heat.

People also use machines to change forms of energy. The cable car in the picture changes electrical energy to energy of motion. The electric toothbrush in the picture stays in a base that has an electric cord that plugs into an outlet. The electrical energy is stored as chemical energy in the toothbrush's battery. The chemical energy changes back to electrical energy and then to energy of motion when the toothbrush is turned on.

Chemical energy changes to electrical energy, which changes to energy of motion as the toothbrush moves.

1. ✓ Checkpoint What form of energy do living things change into mechanical energy and thermal energy?

2. Math in Science Food energy is measured in Calories. John eats 2,000 Calories in food in a day. How many Calories does he eat in a week?

363

Ways That Energy Travels

Energy can travel from one place to another. A moving object, such as a baseball, carries energy. You feel the energy when you try to catch the ball. You can tell how much energy the ball has by how hard it hits your hand.

Energy can also travel as waves. Have you ever seen waves of water? These waves carry energy as the baseball does. These waves of energy have the same shape as the waves of a moving rope. Look at the rope on the next page. How would you describe it? Notice that parts of the rope take turns going from side to side. Energy causes this effect as it travels from one end of the rope to the other. The rope itself does not travel forward. Light and certain other forms of kinetic energy move as waves.

Waves in water can be as small as the ripples in the bucket below. Waves caused by hurricanes can be huge. How big the wave is depends on how much energy it carries.

Ocean waves carry energy.

PLOP!

The energy from the falling drop moves in waves across the water. As the waves move away from the source, they lose strength.

Parts of a Wave

You can measure the amount of energy that a wave carries. Look again at the waving rope. One way to measure a wave's energy is by measuring the distance from the midpoint of the wave. The bottom of the wave is called a *trough*. The top of the wave is called a *crest*. Waves with greater distance from the midpoint have more energy. Waves with lesser distance have less energy.

Another way to measure a wave's energy is by measuring the length of the wave. The length of a wave can be the distance from the top of one crest to the top of the next crest. Shorter waves have more energy. Longer waves have less energy.

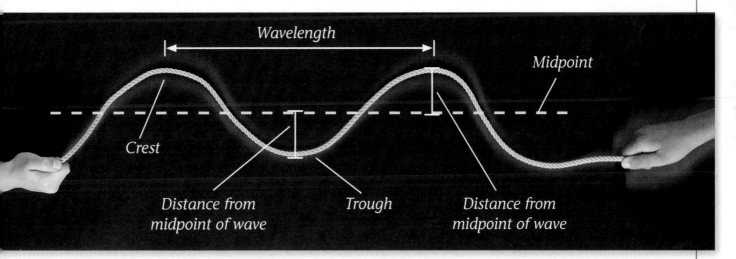

Wavelength

Midpoint

Crest

Distance from midpoint of wave

Trough

Distance from midpoint of wave

✓ Lesson Checkpoint

1. Name two types of energy that travel in waves.

2. What happens to energy as it travels away from the source?

3. **Main Idea and Details** Read the paragraph at the top of this page. Use a graphic organizer. What is the main idea? What are the supporting details?

Moving a loose rope from side-to-side on a table makes energy move forward along the rope in the form of waves. The rope itself does not travel forward.

What is heat energy?

Matter contains thermal energy. Thermal energy travels through objects and space as heat. Heat travels from warm objects to cool ones until they are both at the same temperature.

Heat Energy

Matter is made of very small, moving particles. Each particle of matter is moving because it has energy. The sun's rays feel warm on your skin, for instance. The sun's rays warm matter by making its particles move faster. The energy of moving particles is called **thermal energy.** Thermal energy is the total energy of all the particles in matter.

Thermal energy moves as heat from a warmer object to a cooler object. Put a spoon into a hot drink. Heat travels from the drink through the cooler spoon. In a short time, the top of the spoon will feel warm. Once the drink and the spoon reach the same temperature, the flow of energy stops.

What will happen to the spoon after it is in the hot liquid for a while?

The fish is in a bag of water at room temperature. It waits for the clean, cold tank water to warm up. Why will the temperature of both soon be the same?

Sources of Heat

When energy is changed from one form to another, at least some heat is given off. The burner coils below the pot change electrical energy to heat. Burning matches, wood, and natural gas are examples of chemical changes that give off heat. You notice friction when you rub your hands together to warm them. The friction caused by rubbing gives off heat. Every time energy moves, there is heat.

OUCH!

Be careful! The chemical change that happens when a match is lit is a source of heat.

1. ✓**Checkpoint** What are four different kinds of heat sources?

2. **Writing** in Science **Expository** Write a paragraph in your **science journal** to explain how energy travels to the vegetables in the pot.

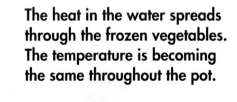

The heat in the water spreads through the frozen vegetables. The temperature is becoming the same throughout the pot.

367

Effects of Heat on Matter

Heat energy affects matter. Think about a cup of liquid water. At 0°C (32°F), however, the water has too little thermal energy to stay in its liquid state. At 0°C, water is a solid like the ice cube stack in the picture.

What happens when you add heat to ice? When the temperature of the air surrounding ice is above 0°C, ice starts to melt and become a liquid. That is what's happening to the ice cubes.

You can measure the effect of heat on matter. To do this, you could chart the time that ice takes to melt. Look again at the stack of ice cubes. At 9 A.M. you put the ice cubes where the temperature remains steady at a certain point above freezing. At 9:15 A.M. what do you observe? Heat moves from the air into the ice. How could you measure the amount of ice that has melted? At 9:30 A.M. what do you observe? Record the time when all the ice is melted. Measure the volume of melted ice. Calculate the amount of time it takes for a certain amount of ice to melt in air of a certain temperature. The time is a rough measure of the change caused by heat energy.

This device shows that the temperature inside and outside a house is about the same. What would happen if the temperature outside dropped to 50°F?

The change from ice to liquid water is related to a change in temperature.

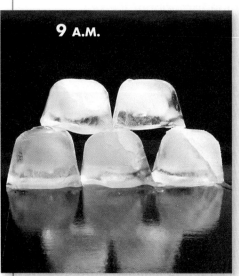

9 A.M.

9:15 A.M.

9:30 A.M.

If more heat is added to water, water evaporates. It becomes the invisible gas called water vapor. At a temperature of 100°C (212°F), heat makes liquid water change in another way. Heat makes the water boil. Look at the bubbling flask of water. Heat at the bottom of the flask makes water expand. Expand means to get bigger. The liquid water expands enough to evaporate and become a hot gas. Very hot bubbles of this gas float to the water's surface. These bubbles break open and release a cloud of hot water droplets.

At 100°C (212°F) heat makes liquid water change in a special way.

Toast Time!
How has heat energy changed this piece of bread?

☑ **Lesson Checkpoint**

1. What is the main source of heat on Earth?

2. What causes matter to be in a solid, liquid, or gas state?

3. **Writing** in Science
Descriptive In your **science journal,** write a paragraph that describes how a campfire keeps campers warm on a cold night.

Burning fuels, such as the gas in this gas lamp, can produce light as well as heat.

Electricity in heat lamps makes heat and light. A heat lamp is keeping this meerkat warm.

What is light energy?

Light is a form of energy. We can see some of the ways that light behaves. Light affects some of the properties of matter.

Sources of Light

The Sun is our main source of energy. The Sun's energy travels from the Sun to Earth as waves. The waves have different amounts of energy. We can see or feel the effects of only some of these waves. Light is energy that we can see.

Chemical changes are another source of light. Burning is a chemical change. Candles, campfires, and matches, for instance, give off light as they burn. The lamp in the picture gives off light as the gas burns. The anglerfish's tentacle gives off light too. Chemical changes in the fish's body produce light.

This anglerfish lives deep in the ocean where there is little light. It makes light to attract food.

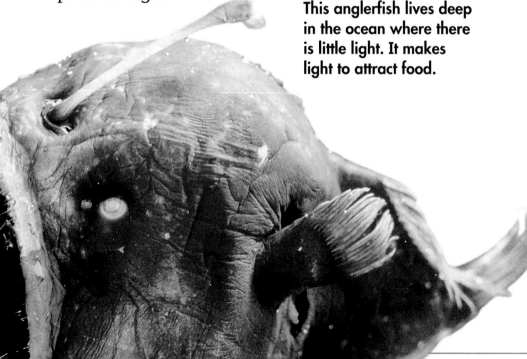

Electricity is also a source of light. It makes the wire in a light bulb get so hot that it glows and gives off light. Most sources of light are also sources of heat. Heat lamps are used to keep things warm.

The Path of Light

Light travels from its source in straight lines in all directions. Light will continue to travel in this way until it is stopped by an object. Light will not bend or turn corners in order to get around objects. That is why objects that block light's path cause shadows. Shadows are areas behind the objects that are not getting direct light. The length of the shadow depends on the angle of the light. The shadows you have cast may have been taller than you really are!

1. **✓ Checkpoint** Name three sources of light energy.

2. **Writing in Science** **Narrative** Write a paragraph in your **science journal** telling about the light sources you have seen today. Include what caused the light.

Why do these tables and chairs make shadows in the sunlight?

How Light Changes

When light hits some objects, much of it can pass through them. These objects do not block all the light. That's why you can see through a window and a clear glass of water.

All objects **reflect** light. This means light bounces off the object and goes in a different direction. Some objects reflect light better than others. Their surfaces are very flat and smooth. All the light that reflects off the surface travels together in the same direction. A mirror reflects light. The light bounces back to your eyes. The smooth lake also reflects light.

What is happening to light in the water droplets in the picture? The droplets **refract,** or bend, the light. When refraction causes the light to bend, the light changes direction. Objects can look different from the way they usually appear. The droplets refract light from the flowers. As the light rays bend, tiny images of the flower form. The lens in a telescope can make big images of small objects. The lens in each of your eyes refracts light too.

The trees are reflected in the smooth water of the lake.

Each water droplet refracts light. A tiny image of the flower forms.

372

Light refracts because it passes through different materials at different speeds. Light passing through air slows down when it enters water. This causes the straw in the glass to look broken.

Sometimes refraction causes light to separate into its many colors. Then you see a rainbow. Water droplets in the air over a sprinkler refract light in the same way.

Light is made up of different colors. When light hits objects, they **absorb,** or take in, some of the light. They reflect the rest. Different objects absorb and reflect different colors of light. If an object looks red in sunlight, it is reflecting red light and absorbing the other colors of light. If an object looks white, it is reflecting all the colors of sunlight. If an object looks black, it is absorbing all the colors of sunlight. Dark objects feel hot in sunlight. A lot of absorbed sunlight turns to heat.

Water causes light to refract, so the straw looks broken.

✔ Lesson Checkpoint

1. What is the main source of light on Earth?

2. How does a shadow form?

3. **Writing** in Science **Narrative**
   Write a story about light in your **science journal.** Use examples of light being absorbed, reflected, and refracted. Brainstorm with others what your story might include.

Effects of Light

Objects can change light. They can reflect, refract, or absorb it. For instance, in sunlight, this chicken looks mostly white. In turn, light can change objects. How is this green light changing the white chicken?

Lesson 5

What is electrical energy?

Matter is made of particles that have electric charges. Electric charges can move as electrical energy through a closed circuit.

Electric Charges

All matter is made up of small particles that have electric charges. An **electric charge** is a tiny amount of energy. Particles have both positive and negative charges. When particles have an equal number of positive and negative charges, they balance each other. The matter has no overall charge. Matter with more negative charges than positive charges has an overall negative charge. Matter with more positive charges than negative charges has an overall positive charge.

A balloon with a balanced charge does not attract the paper pieces.

Lightning is a result of moving electric charges.

What happens when matter with a negative charge is near matter with a positive charge? The positive and negative charges attract. The negative charge travels toward matter that has a positive charge. If you get a shock when you touch someone, negative charges have jumped between you and that person. Lightning is the result of a much bigger jump of electric charges. Lightning happens when negative electric charges travel within clouds or between clouds and the ground. Light, heat, and sound energy are given off.

The attraction between positive and negative charges can cause objects to stick together. Charges that are the same can cause objects to push away from each other. Rubbing a balloon on your hair, for instance, causes it to pick up negative charges from your hair. The extra negative charge on the balloon pushes aside the negative charges on one side of a piece of paper. This leaves the side of paper closest to the balloon with a positive charge. The balloon then attracts the positive side of the paper. The paper sticks to the balloon.

Rubbing two balloons on your hair gives both balloons the same charge. The balloons then push apart from each other.

Rubbing the balloon gives it an electric charge. It attracts objects with the opposite charge. It pushes away from objects with the same charge.

1. ✓**Checkpoint**   What causes lightning?

2. **Art** in Science   Draw a picture of two balloons that shows what happens when one balloon has a positive charge and the other balloon has a negative charge.

Electric Currents and Circuits

Electric current is the movement of electrical energy or electric charge from one place to another. Lightning is an uncontrolled electric current. Lightning can travel in any direction. To be useful, an electric current must travel in a planned way through wires or other materials. This way, electric current can turn on lights or make a CD player work.

Batteries or an outlet that you can plug a cord into are good sources of electrical energy. The path that a controlled electric current flows through is an **electric circuit.** The path must be unbroken for the energy to flow through it. Find the switch in the picture. The switch is on, or closed, so the circuit is unbroken. Electrical energy can flow through the wires of the circuit. If the switch was off, or open, the current could not flow through the circuit.

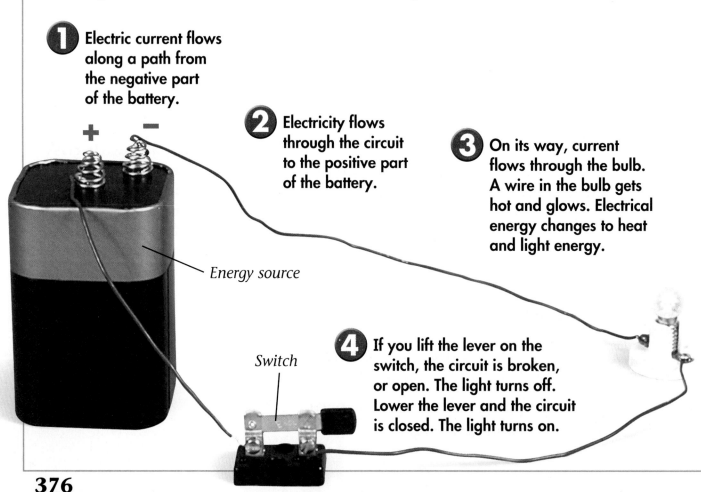

1 Electric current flows along a path from the negative part of the battery.

2 Electricity flows through the circuit to the positive part of the battery.

3 On its way, current flows through the bulb. A wire in the bulb gets hot and glows. Electrical energy changes to heat and light energy.

Energy source

Switch

4 If you lift the lever on the switch, the circuit is broken, or open. The light turns off. Lower the lever and the circuit is closed. The light turns on.

How Electrical Energy Changes Form

	Light	Electricity passes through bulbs of all kinds. Bulbs change electrical energy to light so we can see at night. Some heat is given off.
	Heat	Electricity passes through coils in heaters. Coils change electrical energy to heat so we can be warm in winter, or cook our food.
	Sound	Electricity passes around a magnet. The magnet changes electrical energy to vibrations of plastic discs in headphone speakers. Then we can hear music.
	Magnetic Force	Electricity passes around a huge magnet. The moving electricity makes a magnetic field that attracts metal containing iron to the magnet. The magnet can be used to lift heavy cars.

We rely on electricity for most of our everyday needs. We therefore spend a great deal of effort changing sources of energy into electricity. We change the power of moving water into electricity. We turn the heat of burning coal into electricity. We even turn sunlight into electricity. What happens to electricity once it gets to our homes? Study the table above. Can you imagine not having electricity?

✓ Lesson Checkpoint

1. What is the difference between a controlled and an uncontrolled electric current? Give an example of each.

2. What happens when an electric circuit is open?

3. **Main Idea and Details** Describe the path of electricity through a simple electric circuit.

Investigate Do freshwater ice and saltwater ice melt the same way?

Materials

2 cups and masking tape

water and graduated cylinder (or measuring cup)

spoon and salt

2 thermometers

tub with very warm water (for Day 2)

timer or stopwatch (or clock with a second hand)

Process Skills

By making careful **observations** of ice melting and by **collecting data** and organizing it into a chart, you learned how salt affects the melting of ice.

What to Do

1 Label one cup *fresh water*. Add 100 mL of water.

2 Label the other cup *salt water*. Add 100 mL of water and 1 spoonful of salt. Stir.

3 Place a thermometer in each cup. Your teacher will put the cups in a freezer overnight.

4 After the water is frozen, record the temperature in each cup.

5 Put both cups in a tub of very warm water. **Observe** the temperature in each cup until all the ice in the cup melts. Record the temperature every minute.

6 Construct a chart or table to help you **collect** your **data**.

Melting Time of Ice

Time (minutes)	Temperature of Salt Water (°C)	Temperature of Fresh Water (°C)
0 (start)		
1		
2		
3		

Make a graph if you think it will better help you interpret the data.

Explain Your Results

1. You put the cups of ice in warm water. This added energy to the frozen water. Heat moved from the warm water to the ice. How did the temperature in each cup change? Look at your chart. Describe the pattern of change.

2. Based on your **observations**, in which cup did the ice finish melting first?

Go Further

How would adding more salt to the water affect how fast the ice would melt? Investigate to find out.

Measuring Temperature

Recording temperature is one way to measure thermal energy. You can use different scales to measure temperature.

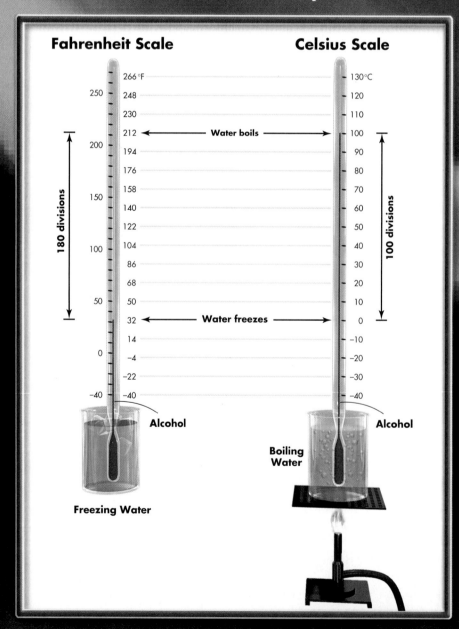

Fahrenheit Scale

266 °F
250   248
      230
      212   ← Water boils →
200   194
      176
      158
150   140
      122
100   104
      86
      68
 50   50
      32   ← Water freezes →
      14
  0   -4
      -22
-40   -40

180 divisions

Alcohol

Freezing Water

Celsius Scale

130 °C
120
110
100
90
80
70
60
50
40
30
20
10
0
-10
-20
-30
-40

100 divisions

Alcohol

Boiling Water

The Celsius scale is often used in science. The Fahrenheit scale is often used in everyday life, such as reading the temperature outdoors. Sometimes both scales are used.

Degrees Celsius is written °C. So 40°C is read "forty degrees Celsius."

Degrees Fahrenheit is written °F. So 40°F is read "forty degrees Fahrenheit."

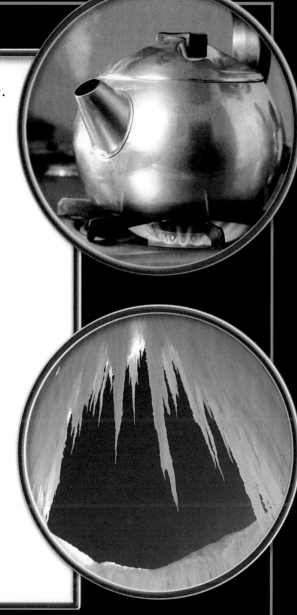

1. What is the boiling point of water on the Celsius scale? What is the boiling point on the Fahrenheit scale?

2. What is the freezing point of water on the Celsius scale? What is the freezing point of water on the Fahrenheit scale?

3. About what is the temperature in degrees Fahrenheit when it is 30°C?

Lab zone Take-Home Activity

Watch the weather report on TV. Are temperatures given in degrees Fahrenheit, Celsius, or both? Make a list of three cities talked about in the report. Write down their temperatures in degrees Fahrenheit and in degrees Celsius. You can use the thermometers shown here.

Chapter 13 Review and Test Prep

Use Vocabulary

absorb (page 373)	**potential energy** (page 360)
electric charge (page 374)	**reflect** (page 372)
electric circuit (page 376)	**refract** (page 372)
electric current (page 376)	**thermal energy** (page 366)
kinetic energy (page 361)	

Use the term from the list above that best completes each sentence.

1. Energy that has the ability to cause a change is _____.

2. A lens causes light to bend or _____.

3. The energy of motion is _____.

4. Objects _____ light that they take in.

5. The path that a controlled electric current flows through is a(n) _____.

6. Two balloons will push away from each other if they have the same _____.

7. Mirrors work because they _____ light.

8. A(n) _____ is the movement of electrical energy from one place to another.

9. The total energy of all the particles in an object is the amount of _____ the object has.

Explain Concepts

10. Explain how to measure the energy in a wave.

11. Describe how light energy travels.

12. If an object has a temperature of 10°C and the air around it is 20°C, will the object gain or lose heat energy? Explain your answer.

Process Skills

13. **Infer** What would happen to the electric current if the part of the light bulb that glows breaks?

14. **Predict** You are having hot soup for lunch. You put a metal spoon in your soup and leave it for a minute. Predict what will happen to the spoon.

Main Idea and Details

15. Make a graphic organizer like the one shown below. Fill in details that support the main idea.

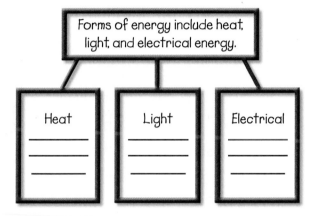

Test Prep

Choose the letter that best completes the statement or answers the question.

16. What kind of energy is stored in a battery?

- (A) kinetic
- (B) light
- (C) chemical
- (D) thermal

17. What color is an object if it reflects blue?

- (F) red
- (G) blue
- (H) yellow
- (I) orange

18. A dark towel that is placed in the sunlight feels warm because it

- (A) reflects the Sun's rays.
- (B) refracts the Sun's rays.
- (C) absorbs the Sun's rays.
- (D) allows the Sun's rays to pass through.

19. Explain why the answer you chose for Question 18 is best. For each of the answers you did not choose, give a reason why it is not the best choice.

20. Writing in Science

Descriptive Write a paragraph that describes different forms of energy.

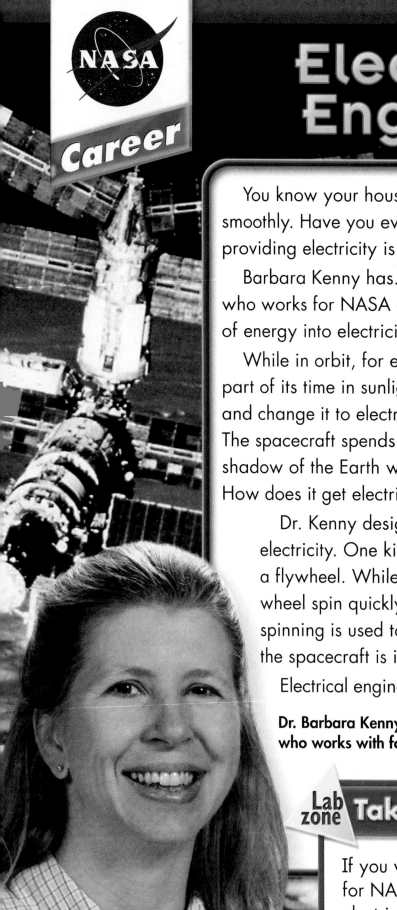

Electrical Engineer

You know your house needs electricity to run smoothly. Have you ever thought about how important providing electricity is during space missions?

Barbara Kenny has. She is an electrical engineer who works for NASA on ways to change other kinds of energy into electricity to run spacecraft.

While in orbit, for example, a spacecraft spends part of its time in sunlight. Solar panels gather light and change it to electricity used to run the ship. The spacecraft spends the rest of its time in the shadow of the Earth where there is no sunlight. How does it get electricity then?

Dr. Kenny designs generators that make electricity. One kind uses a heavy wheel called a flywheel. While in sunlight, motors make this wheel spin quickly. The kinetic energy from spinning is used to generate electricity while the spacecraft is in the dark.

Electrical engineers obtain a college degree.

Dr. Barbara Kenny is an engineer who works with forms of energy.

Lab zone Take-Home Activity

If you were an electrical engineer for NASA, what special kind of electrical equipment would you design? How would it be used?

Chapter 14
Sound

You Will Discover

- how different kinds of sound are produced.
- how sound energy and matter interact.
- how sound travels through different materials.

online
Student Edition
sfsuccessnet.com

How does energy produce the sounds we hear?

vibration

pitch

Chapter 14 Vocabulary

vibration page 392

pitch page 392

compression wave page 396

compression wave

Explore How can you see sound vibrations?

Hold your fingers on your throat. Speak. When you speak, air from your lungs moves past your vocal cords. Feel the vibrations caused by your vocal cords.

Materials

safety goggles

cup

plastic wrap

rubber band

salt

metric ruler

What to Do

1 Make a vibration viewer.

Be careful!

Wear safety goggles.

Sprinkle a little salt on top.

Tightly cover a cup with plastic wrap. Hold it on with a rubber band.

2 Look down at the cup from 3 cm away. Talk softly and loudly. Use a high pitch and a low pitch. Observe how loudness and pitch affect what the salt does.

Optional: If musical instruments are available, observe the vibrations made as you blow, pluck, or tap a musical instrument. Discuss and compare the ways you change pitch and the ways the vibrations change.

Explain Your Results

Collect Data Make a chart to show what you **observed**.

How to Read Science

Compare and Contrast

When you **compare** things, you tell how they are alike. When you **contrast** things, you tell how they are different.

- Writers sometimes use clue words such as *similar*, *alike*, *all*, *both*, or *in the same way* when they compare things.
- Writers sometimes use clue words such as *different*, *unlike*, or *in a different way* when they contrast things.

You can use what you have already **observed** about how instruments sound to help you compare and contrast.

Advertisement

Sound Machines

All our instruments are alike in one way. Vibrate them and you'll get music! But the sounds and how they are made are very different. How are the sounds alike and different? Come try them out!

Apply It!

The advertisement above asks you to **compare and contrast.** Tell how the sounds of the instruments are alike and different. Use a graphic organizer to compare and contrast.

Different   Alike   Different

389

🔊 You Are There!

You are in the middle of a huge celebration.
Everyone is watching the parade and listening
to the marching bands. Thousands of people
are in the crowd. Horns are honking. People
are cheering. You know that later, after
it's dark, the fireworks will make different
sounds. What's the reason for all this sound?
It's the Fourth of July!

🔊 AudioText 🔊

Lesson 1

What causes sounds?

Sounds are all around you. You enjoy some sounds, like music. But other sounds hurt your ears. All sounds are made when matter moves.

Noisemakers like these are sometimes used on New Year's Eve. What kind of sounds do they make?

Suppose you are taking a walk in a city. You might hear the loud sounds of car horns and garbage trucks. You might hear the soft sound of your friend's voice. If you are taking a walk in the country, you might hear the loud sounds of farm tractors. You might also hear cows mooing. In a forest, you might hear the soft sounds of water trickling in a creek and the sounds of birds chirping.

Some of these sounds might be pleasant to you. Others might bother you. Some noises, like the sound of a jet plane taking off, might even hurt your ears. The sounds we hear every day are different. Yet all sounds are alike in some ways.

1. ✓**Checkpoint** Describe some ways that sounds are alike and different.

2. **Writing in Science** **Descriptive** In your **science journal,** write two paragraphs about the sounds you hear every day. Tell why you think the sounds are pleasant or unpleasant.

A tambourine makes sounds when you hit it with your hand or shake it.

The Causes of Sound

Sounds happen when matter moves back and forth very quickly. A back-and-forth movement is called a **vibration.** Sounds happen only when something vibrates.

Suppose you are listening to these instruments being played. You would hear high sounds and low sounds. **Pitch** describes how high or low a sound is. Objects that vibrate slowly make sounds with a low pitch. Objects that vibrate more quickly make sounds with a higher pitch.

When a drum or cymbal is struck, it vibrates and makes a sound. Different sizes and shapes of drums produce sounds with different pitches.

SciLinks Take It to the Net
sfsuccessnet.com

keyword: vibration
code: g3p392

Hitting or Plucking to Make Sound

Percussion instruments make sound when they are hit. Steel drums are played by tapping them with a rubber hammer. Other drums are played with wooden sticks, metal brushes, or the hands.

If you lightly tapped a drum, you would hear a soft sound. If you hit the drum harder, you would hear a louder sound. The harder you hit the drum, the farther the drumhead moves back and forth. The vibrations become stronger. The loudness of the sound depends on the strength of the vibrations.

Stringed instruments make sound when the strings are plucked or when a bow is rubbed across the strings. The pitch of the sound each string makes depends on how long, thick, and tightly stretched it is. The short, thin, and tight strings make faster vibrations. So the sounds they make have higher pitches.

When a musician plucks the harp strings, they vibrate. The vibrations make sound.

This instrument makes sounds when it is hit with a rubber hammer. The vibrations of the blocks make sounds.

1. ✓**Checkpoint** How is sound made?

2. 🎯 **Compare and Contrast**
   How are the sounds produced by different strings of a harp alike and different?

393

Using Air to Make Sound

Place your fingers lightly across your throat. Then hum. Can you feel your vocal cords vibrate?

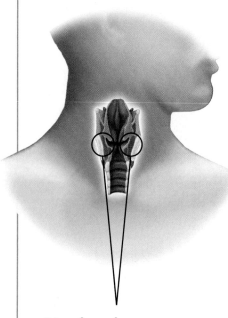

Vocal cords are two pairs of thin tissue in the windpipe.

The trumpet makes sounds when the player blows air into it. The player's lips vibrate against the mouthpiece of the trumpet.

The sound of your voice also comes from vibrations. You are able to speak and sing because your vocal cords vibrate. When you speak, your vocal cords tighten. They vibrate as air passes between them. The tighter your vocal cords get, the higher the pitch of your voice becomes.

Wind instruments make sounds when air inside them vibrates. You make sounds with a trumpet by blowing into it and vibrating your lips. This makes the air inside the trumpet vibrate also.

You can change the pitch of a trumpet's sound in two ways. One way is to change how your lips vibrate. The other way is to press on the valves of the trumpet. This changes the length of the vibrating air column inside the trumpet.

An oboe is also a wind instrument. It has a double reed at the top. A reed is a thin piece of wood. The player blows on the reeds, making them vibrate. This vibration makes the air inside the oboe vibrate and make a sound. Pressing keys on the oboe changes the pitch of the sound.

A harmonica has several metal reeds that vibrate when a person blows air across them.

A saxophone has a longer air column than a clarinet. So the sounds it makes have lower pitches than the sounds a clarinet can make.

A clarinet uses a single wooden reed like this one. The reed presses on the player's lower lip and vibrates when the player blows air across it.

This clarinet produces its lowest note when all the holes are covered. Uncovering the last hole makes the air column shorter. Then the pitch of the sound is higher.

✓ **Lesson Checkpoint**

1. What makes the vocal cords vibrate?

2. What are two ways that sounds can be different?

3. **Writing in Science** **Descriptive** Write a paragraph in your **science journal** describing how guitar strings with different lengths make music with different sounds.

395

Lesson 2

How does sound travel?

Sound travels through matter. You can hear the sound of a fire engine several blocks away. But if you were on the Moon, you would not be able to hear anything. The Moon has no atmosphere, and sound can travel only through matter.

Sound waves from a megaphone spread out in all directions. They travel through the air.

What Are Sound Waves?

The energy of back-and-forth vibrations makes sound. Think about the sound of a bell that startles you, for example. As the bell rings, its vibrations result in spaces where air particles are squeezed together and spaces where air particles are spread apart. This movement of particles makes a kind of wave called a **compression wave.** Sound waves are compression waves.

Sound waves travel through matter like energy travels through a coiled spring. Particles that make up matter along the way take turns being squeezed together and spread apart. The length of a sound wave is its wavelength. It is measured from the center of one compression to the center of the next compression.

These bells make sounds only when they vibrate.

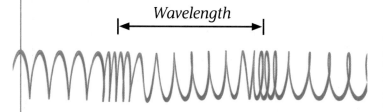

Wavelength

Find the places where the coils in the spring are squeezed together. Find the places where the coils are spread apart. Sound waves carry energy from one place to another in this way.

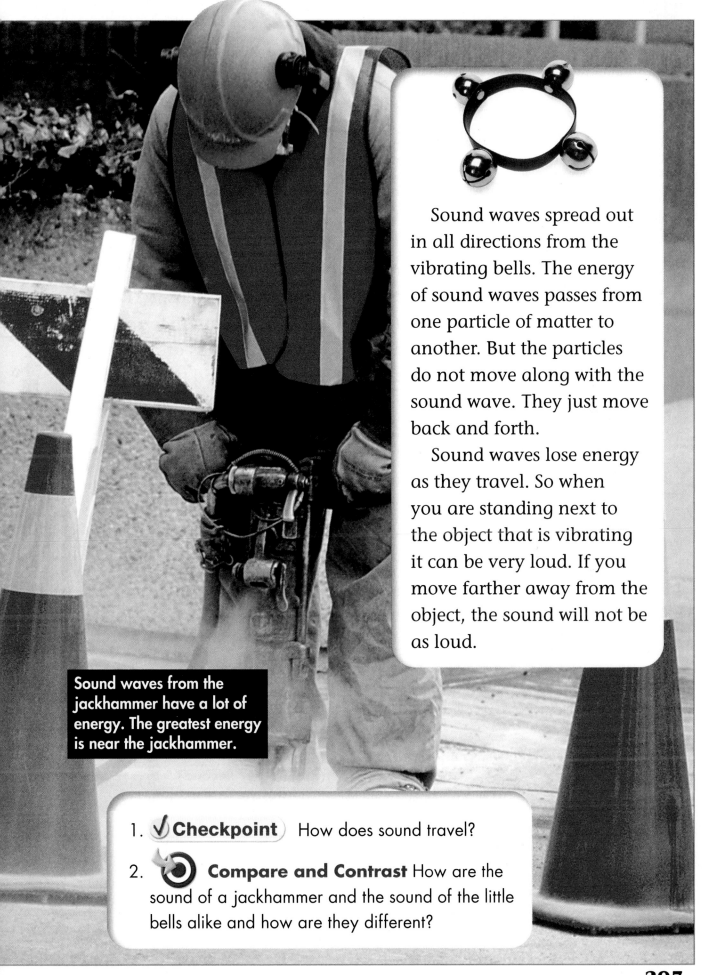

Sound waves spread out in all directions from the vibrating bells. The energy of sound waves passes from one particle of matter to another. But the particles do not move along with the sound wave. They just move back and forth.

Sound waves lose energy as they travel. So when you are standing next to the object that is vibrating it can be very loud. If you move farther away from the object, the sound will not be as loud.

Sound waves from the jackhammer have a lot of energy. The greatest energy is near the jackhammer.

1. ✔ Checkpoint How does sound travel?

2. Compare and Contrast How are the sound of a jackhammer and the sound of the little bells alike and how are they different?

The speed of sound through air is about 340 meters per second. So you would hear the sound of this bell in less than $\frac{1}{100}$ second if you were in the same room.

The particles in solids, generally, are the closest together. So sound waves travel quickest in solids. When you use a tin-can telephone, sound waves travel quickly through the string from one can to the other.

Sound and Matter

You can hear sound only when it travels through matter. Since there is no matter between stars and planets in outer space, there is no sound there. Sound moves through solids, liquids, and gases. The speed of a sound wave depends on what kind of matter it is traveling through.

Air is made of gases. The particles in gases are farther apart than in liquids and solids. So it takes longer for one gas particle to hit another and move the energy along. Particles in liquids are closer together. Water is a liquid. So sound travels more quickly in water than it does in air. Particles in solids are closer together than in liquids, so sound travels quickest in solids.

You hear an echo when sound waves strike an object and then bounce back. Sonar equipment uses echoes to study the ocean. A ship sends out sound waves to the ocean bottom. Equipment measures how long it takes for the sound to bounce back. Sound waves travel about 1,530 meters per second in seawater. Knowing this, scientists can find the depth of the ocean in a certain place.

Speed of Sound	
Material	**Speed (meters per second)**
Solid—Steel	5,200
Liquid—Seawater	1,530
Gas—Air	340

If you are watching fireworks from far away, you often see the flash before you hear the sound. That is because light travels much faster than sound.

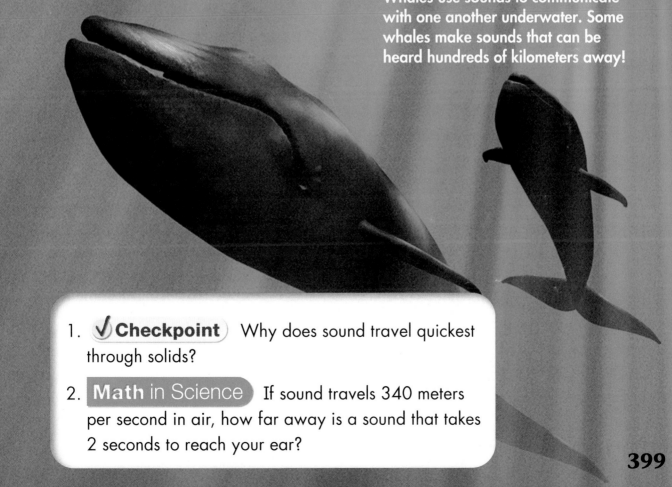

Whales use sounds to communicate with one another underwater. Some whales make sounds that can be heard hundreds of kilometers away!

1. ✓Checkpoint Why does sound travel quickest through solids?

2. Math in Science If sound travels 340 meters per second in air, how far away is a sound that takes 2 seconds to reach your ear?

399

The Ear

We hear sounds because of our ears. Our ears receive sound waves. The waves travel along a path toward our brain. The brain receives signals that we recognize as sounds.

Eardrum
Inside the ear, the sound waves hit the eardrum. The eardrum is a thin, skin-like layer stretched across the inside of the ear. When sound hits the eardrum, it begins to vibrate.

Little Bones
Three tiny bones touch the eardrum. When the eardrum vibrates, it makes these bones vibrate. These bones are part of the middle part of the ear.

Outer Ear
The part of the ear that you can see collects sound waves traveling in air.

Humans cannot hear some of the sounds that other animals can hear.

Inner Ear
The inner ear has a part that is shaped like a shell. It is filled with liquid. The movement of the tiny bones makes tiny hairs in the liquid vibrate. The hairs are attached to nerves that carry signals to the brain. This is how we hear.

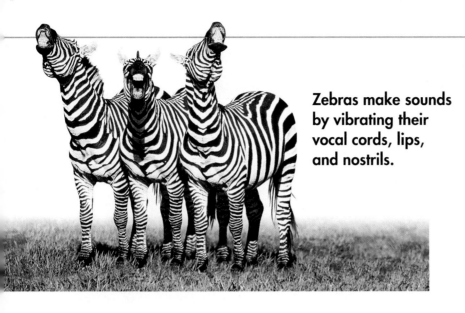

Zebras make sounds by vibrating their vocal cords, lips, and nostrils.

Many kinds of insects make sounds by rubbing body parts together. This katydid makes chirping sounds by rubbing its wings together.

Most people know the sounds made when animals vibrate their vocal cords. Most have heard a dog's bark or a cow's moo. But not all animals make sounds by using only vocal cords. Woodpeckers use their beaks to tap out sounds on tree trunks. The vibrating wings of bees and mosquitoes make buzzing sounds.

Some bats send out high-pitched clicking sounds that people cannot hear. These sounds bounce off insects and return to the bats' ears. This is how bats find their food.

A male seal can roar loudly at other males. Seals use sound to defend their resources.

✓ **Lesson Checkpoint**

1. What path do sound waves follow through the ear?

2. How do some insects make sounds?

3. **Art** in Science   Draw a picture of a musical instrument or an animal making a sound. Label your drawing to tell how the sound is made and how it travels.

Chimpanzees make many different sounds. They grunt, bark, squeak, scream, and even laugh.

401

Investigate How well does sound travel through different materials?

Materials

resealable plastic bags

block of wood

water

unsharpened pencil

What to Do

1 Prepare the bags.

Fill a bag with air by blowing into it. Seal tightly.

Fill another bag $\frac{1}{2}$ full with water. Squeeze out any air. Seal tightly.

Put the block of wood into a third bag. Squeeze out any air. Seal tightly.

Process Skills

You **infer** when you use your **observations** to put materials in order from best to poorest carrier of sound.

2 If necessary, roll down the top of the bag to make it puff up. Hold it against your ear. Cover your other ear with your hand. Listen as your partner taps the bag gently with the pencil eraser. Then repeat the test using the bag with water and the bag with wood.

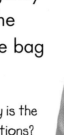

What part of your body is the receiver of sound vibrations?

3 Compare the sounds you heard. Record your **observations**. Which was loudest? Which was softest?

How Well Sound Travels Through Different Materials

Material	Observations (soft, louder, loudest)
air (gas)	
water (liquid)	
wood (solid)	

Explain Your Results

1. Did the tapping seem loudest through air (gas), water (liquid), or wood (solid)?
2. **Infer** Compare how well sound travels through different materials. Arrange the materials in order from the best carrier of sound to the poorest carrier of sound.

┌─ **Go Further** ─
How can you use a sound recorder to help collect data about the way sound travels through different materials? Make a plan to investigate.

403

Math in Science

Comparing Speeds of Sound

You know that sound waves travel at different speeds through different types of matter. Sound travels most slowly through gases and most quickly through solids. But what about the same kind of matter? Does sound travel through plastic and through steel at different speeds, even though they are both solids?

The table below shows that sound waves travel at different speeds through different solids. For example, sound travels at 2,680 meters per second through silver. Sound travels almost twice that speed through steel. Out of all the solids in the table, sound travels most slowly through plastic.

Speed of Sound through Solids	
Material	**Speed** (meters per second)
Plastic	1,800
Silver	2,680
Gold	3,240
Copper	3,560
Brick	3,650
Oak wood	3,850
Glass	4,540
Iron	5,130
Steel	5,200

🖥 ⓔ **Tools** Take It to the Net
sfsuccessnet.com

Sound also travels at different speeds through the same material at different temperatures. The table below shows the speed of sound through air at different temperatures. Use the table to answer the questions.

Speed of Sound through Air	
Air Temperature (°C)	Speed (meters per second)
0	332
10	338
20	343
30	349

1 At which temperature do sound waves travel most slowly through air?

A. 0°C   B. 10°C   C. 20°C   D. 30°C

2 How much more quickly do sound waves travel through air at 20°C than at 0°C?

F. $8 \frac{m}{s}$ G. $11 \frac{m}{s}$ H. $13 \frac{m}{s}$ I. $14 \frac{m}{s}$

3 During which season do you think sound travels most quickly in air?

A. spring   B. summer   C. fall   D. winter

Lab zone Take-Home Activity

Find a very thick book. Hold the book against one ear while someone taps the other side of the book. Do you hear the sound with your ear touching the book before you hear it with your other ear? Explain the difference.

Chapter 14 Review and Test Prep

Use Vocabulary

compression wave (page 396)	**pitch** (page 392)
	vibration (page 392)

Use the term from the list above that best completes each sentence.

1. _____ describes how high or low a sound is.

2. A back-and-forth movement that causes sound is called a _____.

3. A sound wave is a kind of _____.

Explaining Concepts

4. How can guitar strings with different lengths make music that has different sounds?

5. Explain how covering your ears can keep you from hearing a sound.

6. Why does sound travel more slowly through air than it does through water?

7. Explain how people make sounds when they talk.

8. Explain how an oboe makes musical sounds.

Process Skills

9. **Infer** what happens if you sprinkle confetti on a drumhead and then hit the drum with a drumstick.

10. Suppose you place a rubber band around a book. You place two pencils under the rubber band to hold it up. Then you pluck the rubber band between the pencils. **Predict** how the pitch of the sound will change when the pencils are moved closer together and then farther apart.

11. The loudness of sounds is measured in units called decibels. Sounds with levels between 60 and 84 decibels can be annoying. Sounds above 85 decibels can harm your hearing. Look at the chart below. **Classify** each sound as annoying or harmful.

Sound	Loudness (in decibels)
Jet plane	150
Lawn mower	80
Rock band	110
Vacuum cleaner	70

406 Mind Point Quiz Show

12. Infer how sonar might be used to protect a ship from going into water that is too shallow.

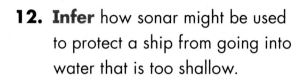

Compare and Contrast

13. Use a graphic organizer to show how the sounds made by a car horn and a song bird are alike and different.

Test Prep

Choose the letter that best completes the statement or answers the question.

14. Which part of the ear collects sound waves?

Ⓐ eardrum   Ⓑ outer ear
Ⓒ nerve   Ⓓ bones

15. Hitting a drum harder will make the sound

Ⓕ louder.
Ⓖ the same.
Ⓗ softer.
Ⓘ lower in pitch.

16. Sound waves travel fastest through

Ⓐ solids.   Ⓑ liquids.
Ⓒ air.   Ⓓ gases.

17. A special nerve inside the head carries messages from the ear to the

Ⓕ eardrum.
Ⓖ brain.
Ⓗ tiny bones.
Ⓘ outer ear.

18. If a guitar string vibrates slowly it will have a pitch that is

Ⓐ high.
Ⓑ soft.
Ⓒ low.
Ⓓ loud.

19. Which instrument is a percussion instrument?

Ⓕ harp
Ⓖ clarinet
Ⓗ trumpet
Ⓘ cymbal

20. Writing in Science

Narrative Suppose that you are a sound wave. Write a story describing how you were produced, how you traveled, and how you were heard.

Dr. Clifton Horne

If you have been in an airport, you know that planes can make a lot of noise. Some scientists are working on ways to make planes quieter. Clifton Horne, NASA Aerospace Engineer, is doing just that.

Dr. Horne uses many microphones and computers to find the direction to the noise source in a jet plane engine and to find out how to make it quieter. Clifton Horne said, "...in the next 10 years we should be able to ... fly on airplanes that people on the ground can see but hardly hear."

While Clifton was growing up he saw many exciting things, such as the Apollo moon landings. He enjoyed hobbies that taught him about astronomy and radio communication. As a result, Clifton decided to become an aerospace engineer.

Dr. Horne says that his English classes, as well as math and science classes, have been very useful in his career. Scientists, including Dr. Horne, spend much time writing and working together in groups. So, the communication skills that Dr. Horne learned in his English classes are very important to him.

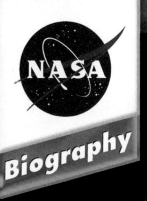

Dr. Clifton Horne uses test engines like the one above in the wind tunnel at NASA's Ames Research Center.

Lab zone Take-Home Activity

People use sound to communicate, to entertain, and to warn of danger. Research a career in industries where sound is important.

Unit C Test Talk

Test-Taking Strategies

Find Important Words

Choose the Right Answer

▶ Use Information from Text and Graphics

Write Your Answer

Use Information from Text and Graphics

Information in text, pictures, and diagrams can help you answer test questions. Read the text and study the graphics. Then answer the questions.

The diagrams show how the particles in solids, liquids, and gases are connected. The captions explain how the particles in solids, liquids, and gases are connected and how they move.

The particles of a solid are firmly connected. They jiggle in place.

The particles of a liquid are loosely connected. They flow past one another.

Gas particles are not connected. They bounce off one another and move freely.

Use What You Know

To answer the questions, find the information in the captions and the graphics. Read each question and decide which answer choice is best.

1. A solid has particles that are
  Ⓐ loosely connected.
  Ⓑ not connected.
  Ⓒ firmly connected.
  Ⓓ connected in pairs.

2. A liquid has particles that
  Ⓕ stay in place.
  Ⓖ flow past one another.
  Ⓗ move freely.
  Ⓘ move in pairs.

3. Which statement describes gas particles?
  Ⓐ They are packed closer together than liquid particles.
  Ⓑ They are firmly connected.
  Ⓒ They are connected in groups.
  Ⓓ They are farther apart than solid or liquid particles.

Unit C Wrap-Up

Chapter 10

What are the properties of matter?

- Matter takes up space, has mass, and has other properties that can be observed.
- Mass, volume, density, and length are some properties of matter that can be measured.

Chapter 11

What are physical and chemical changes in matter?

- Matter can change in its size, shape, or state during a physical change.
- During a chemical change, matter changes into new kinds of matter.

Chapter 12

How do forces cause motion and get work done?

- Forces cause a change in motion and work to be done by changing an object's speed or direction.
- Contact forces change motion only by touching objects. The forces of gravity and magnetism can change an object's motion without touching it.

Chapter 13

How does energy change form?

- Potential energy can change to kinetic energy and kinetic energy can change to potential energy.
- Energy can transfer between the forms of light, electrical, thermal, sound, chemical, mechanical, and magnetic energy.

Chapter 14

How does energy produce the sounds we hear?

- Sound is produced by the energy of vibrating matter traveling as compression waves.
- The pitch of a sound depends on how fast an object vibrates.

Performance Assessment
Identify Electric Charges

Use a wool cloth and balloons to show what happens when objects have different charges. What happens when you move two balloons with no charge toward each other? How can you make a balloon negatively charged? What happens when you move a negatively charged balloon toward a balloon with no charge?

Read More About Physical Science!

Look for books like these in the library.

Experiment How does energy affect the distance a toy car travels?

When you pull back a pullback car, you wind it up. You give it potential energy. When you let it go, the potential energy changes to kinetic energy as the car begins to move. In this activity, you will find out how a car's potential energy affects the distance the car can travel.

Materials

meterstick

pullback toy car

masking tape

Ask a question.

How does a car's potential energy affect the distance it can travel?

State a hypothesis.

If a pullback car's potential energy is greater, then will the distance it travels increase, decrease, or remain about the same? Write your **hypothesis**.

Identify and control variables.

You will change the potential energy your toy car has just before it begins to move. You do this by changing the distance you pull the car back. You will measure the distance the car travels. Everything else must stay the same.

Process Skills

The basis of an **experiment** is a **hypothesis**, a testable **prediction** that helps guide the experiment.

Test your hypothesis.

1 Make a starting line with masking tape.

2 Put down another piece of tape and mark it at 0, 5, 10, 15, 20, 25, and 30 cm.

③ Put the front of the car at the 5 cm line.

④ Pull the car back until the front of the car is at the starting line and let the car go.

⑤ **Measure** the distance the car travels. Record the distance.

⑥ Repeat steps 3 to 5, but use the 10, 15, 20, 25, and 30 cm lines. Record your data each time.

What happens to the car's potential energy when you let go? What happens to its speed as it travels? What causes the car to stop?

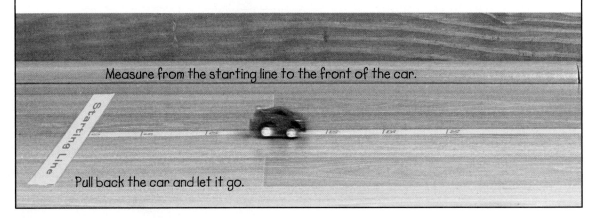

Measure from the starting line to the front of the car.

Pull back the car and let it go.

Collect and record your data.

Distance Moved by Pullback Car	
Distance Pulled Back (cm)	**Distance Traveled** (cm)
0	0
5	
10	
15	
20	
25	
30	

Find a pattern in your chart or graph. Make a prediction based on the evidence. How far would your car go if you pulled it back 35 cm? You might wish to test your prediction.

Interpret your data.

Use your data to make a bar graph. Look at your graph closely. Did the number of centimeters you pulled the car back affect the distance it traveled? Explain. Describe the evidence for your explanation.

How does evidence differ from opinion?

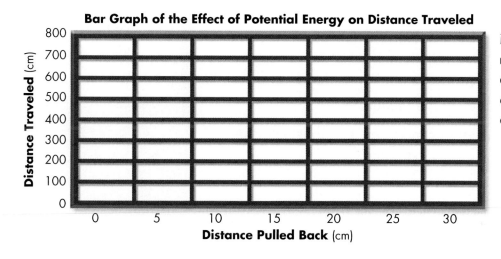

Bar Graph of the Effect of Potential Energy on Distance Traveled

Distance Traveled (cm) — 800, 700, 600, 500, 400, 300, 200, 100, 0

Distance Pulled Back (cm) — 0, 5, 10, 15, 20, 25, 30

Discuss your results with others and consider their explanations.

State your conclusion.

How does increasing a car's potential energy affect the distance it travels? Compare your hypothesis with your results. **Communicate** your conclusion.

Go Further

Suppose you add more mass to the car. How would this affect the distances it travels? Make a prediction. Make and carry out a plan to answer this or another question you may have.

Full Inquiry

Using Scientific Methods

1. Ask a question.
2. State a hypothesis.
3. Identify/control variables.
4. Test your hypothesis.
5. Collect and record your data.
6. Interpret your data.
7. State your conclusion.
8. Go further.

Comparing Density

Matter that has less density than water has buoyancy—it will float in water.

Idea: Compare the density of objects with that of water. Use a container of water and a variety of objects.

Separating Mixtures

The best way to separate a mixture depends on the kinds of matter in the mixture.

Idea: Use a variety of mixtures. Demonstrate the best way to separate each mixture.

Changing Potential to Kinetic Energy

Energy can be stored as potential energy and released as kinetic energy.

Idea: Use a wind-up toy to show how the amount of potential energy affects the distance the toy can travel.

Making Sounds

Sounds vary depending on the way matter vibrates.

Idea: Show how sound changes. Stretch rubber bands of varied sizes across the opening of a box.

EC NTL 10 9 8 7 6 5 4 3

Metric and Customary Measurement

The metric system is the measurement system most commonly used in science. Metric units are sometimes called SI units. SI stands for International System because these units are used around the world.

These prefixes are used in the metric system:

kilo- means *thousand*
1 kilometer equals 1,000 meters
centi- means *hundredths*
100 centimeters equals 1 meter
milli- means one-*thousandth*
1,000 millimeters equals 1 meter

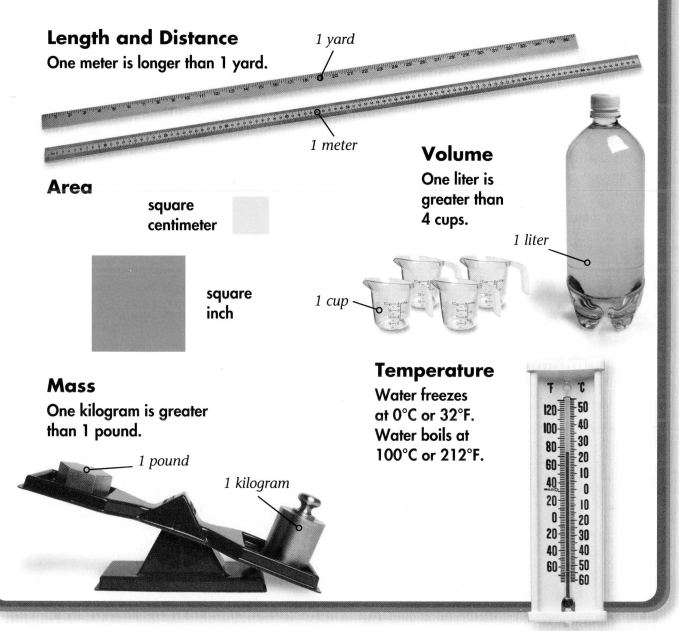

Length and Distance
One meter is longer than 1 yard.

1 yard

1 meter

Area

square centimeter

square inch

Volume
One liter is greater than 4 cups.

1 liter

1 cup

Mass
One kilogram is greater than 1 pound.

1 pound

1 kilogram

Temperature
Water freezes at 0°C or 32°F. Water boils at 100°C or 212°F.

Glossary

The glossary uses letters and signs to show how words are pronounced. The mark ′ is placed after a syllable with a primary or heavy accent. The mark ′ is placed after a syllable with a secondary or lighter accent.

To hear these words pronounced, listen to the AudioText CD.

absorb (ab sôrb′) to take in (p. 373)

adaptation (ad′ ap tā′ shən) trait that helps a living thing survive in its environment (p. 48)

asteroid (as′tə roid′) a small chunk of rock that orbits around the Sun (p. 457)

atmosphere (at′mə sfir) the blanket of air and gases that surround the Earth (p. 176)

atom (at′əm) one of the tiny particles that make up all of matter (p. 282)

axis (ak′sis) an imaginary line around which Earth spins (p. 424)

blizzard (bliz′ərd) a winter storm with very low temperatures, strong winds, heavy snowfall, and blowing snow (p. 183)

buoyancy (boi′ən sē) force exerted on an object that is immersed in a gas or liquid that tends to make it float (p. 286)

carnivore (kär′nə vôr) living things that hunt other animals for food (p. 106)

cause (kȯz) why something happens (p. 277, 311)

change of state (chānj uv stāt) physical change that takes place when matter changes from one state to another (p. 304)

chemical change (kem′ə kəl chānj) a change that causes one kind of matter to become a different kind of matter (p. 311)

classifying (klas′ə fī′ing) to arrange or sort objects, events, or living things according to their properties (p. 244)

collecting data (kə lek′ ting dā′ tə) to gather observations and measurements into graphs, tables or charts (p. 26)

communicating (kə myü′ nə kāt′ ing) using words, pictures, charts, graphs, and diagrams to share information (p. 324)

community (kəm myü′ nə tē) all the populations that live together in the same place (p. 74)

compare (kəm pâr′) to show how things are alike (p. 5, 245, 389, 453)

competition (kom′ pə tish′ən) struggle that happens when two or more living things need the same resource (p. 110)

compression wave (kəm presh′ən wāv) wave that has spaces where particles are squeezed together and spaces where particles are spread apart (p. 396)

computer (kəm pyü′ tər) tool which stores, processes, and gets electronic information (p. 485)

conclusion (kən klü′ zhən) decision reached after considering facts and details (p. 101)

condensation (kon′ den sā′ shən) the changing of a gas into a liquid (p. 157)

coniferous tree (kō nif′ər əs trē) does not lose its needle-like leaves in the fall (p. 16)

conservation (kon′ sər vā′ shən) the saving and wise use of natural resources (p. 250)

constellation (kon′ stə lā′ shən) a group of stars that make a pattern or shape (p. 438)

consumer (kən sü′ mər) living things that eat food (p. 106)

contrast (kən trast′) to show how things are different (p. 5, 245, 389, 453)

core (kôr) the innermost layer of Earth (p. 223)

crust (krust) the outermost layer of Earth (p. 223)

decay (di kā′) to break down, or rot (p. 118, 206)

deciduous (di sij′ü əs) loses its leaves in the fall and grows new ones in the spring (p. 14)

decomposer (dē′kəm pō′zər) a living thing that breaks down waste and things that have died (p. 118)

density (den′sə tē) measure of the amount of matter in a certain amount of space (p. 286)

desert (dez′ərt) an ecosystem that gets less than 25 cm of rainfall a year (p. 78)

details (di tālz′) individual pieces of information that support a main idea (p. 69, 357)

disease (də zēz′) the name we give an illness (p. 126)

earthquake (ėrth′kwāk′) a shaking of Earth's crust caused by sudden, shifting movements in the crust (p. 228)

ecosystem (ē′kō sis′təm) all the living and nonliving things that interact with each other in a given area (p. 72)

effect (ə fekt′) what happens as the result of a cause (p. 149, 277)

electric charge (i lek′trik chärj) tiny amount of energy in the particles of matter (p. 374)

electric circuit (i lek′trik sėr′kit) the path that a controlled electric current flows through (p. 376)

electric current (i lek′trik kėr′ənt) the movement of an electric charge from one place to another (p. 376)

element (el′ə mənt) matter that has only one kind of atom (p. 282)

energy (en′ ər jē) the ability to do work or to cause a change (p. 359)

environment (en vī′rən mənt) everything that surrounds a living thing (p. 71)

equator (i kwā′ tər) the imaginary line that separates the north and south halves of Earth (p. 429)

erosion (i rō′ zhən) the movement of weathered materials (p. 232)

estimating and measuring (es′tə māt ing and mezh′ər ing) to tell what you think an object's measurements are and then to measure it in units (p. 210)

evaporation (i vap′ ə rā′ shən) the changing of a liquid into a gas (p. 157)

experiment (ek sper′ə ment) to formulate and test a hypothesis using a scientific method (p. 140)

explore (ek splôr′) to study a scientific idea in a hands-on manner (p. 36)

extinct (ek stingkt′) no longer lives on Earth (p. 23)

food chain (füd chān) the movement of energy from one type of living thing to another (p. 108)

food web (füd web) the flow of energy between food chains which ties a community together (p. 108)

force (fôrs) a push or a pull (p. 332)

forming questions and hypotheses (fôrm′ing kwes′chənz and hī poth′ə sēz′) to think of how you can solve a problem or answer a question (p. 140)

fossil (fos′ əl) remains or mark of a living thing from long ago (p. 22)

friction (frik′ shən) a contact force that opposes the motion of an object (p. 333)

gas (gas) the form of matter which has no shape, has particles that are not connected to each other, and takes up whatever space is available (p. 281)

germinate (jėr′ mə nāt) begins to grow (p. 20)

germs (jėrmz) small living things that include bacteria and viruses, many of which can cause illness (p. 126)

grassland (gras′ land′) land ecosystem that has many grasses and few trees (p. 76)

gravity (grav′ə tē) a non-contact force that pulls objects toward each other (p. 336)

groundwater (ground′ wȯ′ tər) water that has slowly made its way through soil and then collects in spaces between underground rock; it is brought to the surface by digging wells (p. 155)

habitat (hab′ə tat) the place where a living thing makes its home (p. 72)

heat (hēt) the transfer of thermal energy from one piece of matter to another (p. 366)

herbivore (ėr′bə vôr) living things that eat only plants (p. 106)

hibernate (hī′bər nāt) to spend winter resting; body systems slow down in order to save energy (p. 52)

hurricane (hėr′ə kān) a huge, strong storm that forms over the ocean (p. 182)

identifying and controlling variables (ī den′tə fī ing and kən trōl′ing vâr′ē ə bəlz) to change one thing, but keep all the other factors the same (p. 40)

igneous rock (ig′nē əs rok′) rock that forms when melted earth materials cool and harden (p. 200)

inclined plane (in klīnd′ plān) a slanting surface that connects a lower level to a higher level (p. 340)

inference (in′fər əns) a conclusion based on facts, experiences, observations, or knowledge (p. 173)

inferring (in fėr′ ing) to draw a conclusion or make a reasonable guess based on what you have learned or what you know (p. 100)

inherited (in her′it əd) passed on from parent to offspring (p. 48)

interpreting data (in tėr′prit ing dā′tə) to use the information you have collected to solve problems or answer questions (p. 26)

invention (in ven′ shən) something that has been made for the first time (p. 479)

investigate (in ves′ tə gāt) to solve a problem or answer a question by following an existing procedure or an original one (p. 26)

investigating and experimenting (in ves′ tə gāt ing and ek sper′ə ment ing) to plan and do an investigation to test a hypothesis or solve a problem (p. 508)

kinetic energy (ki net′ik en′ər jē) energy of motion (p. 361)

landform (land′ fôrm) a natural feature on the surface of Earth's crust (p. 224)

larva (lär′ və) stage in an insect's life after it hatches from the egg (p. 45)

lava (lä′ və) hot, molten rock on Earth's surface (p. 226)

lever (lev′ər) a simple machine used to lift and move things (p. 341)

life cycle (līf sī′kəl) the stages through which an organism passes between birth and death (p. 44)

light (līt) a form of energy that can be seen (p. 370)

liquid (lik′wid) matter that does not have a definite shape but takes up a definite amount of space (p. 280)

loam (lōm) soil that contains a mixture of humus and mineral materials of sand, silt, and clay (p. 209)

lunar eclipse (lü′nər i klips′) Earth's shadow moving across the Moon (p. 434)

magma (mag′mə) hot, molten rock that forms deep underground (p. 226)

magnetic (mag net′ik) having the property to pull on, or attract, metals that have iron in them (p. 337)

magnetism (mag′nə tiz′əm) a non-contact force that pulls objects containing iron (p. 337)

main idea (mān ī dē′ə) what a paragraph is about; the most important idea (p. 69, 357)

making operational definitions (māk′ ing op′ə rā′ shən əl def′ə nish′ənz) to define or describe an object or event based on your own experience (p. 68)

making and using models (māk′ ing and yüz′ ing mod′lz) to make a model from materials or to make a sketch or a diagram (p. 36)

mantle (man′tl) the middle layer of Earth (p. 223)

mass (mas) amount of matter (p. 284)

matter (mat′ər) anything that takes up space and has mass (p. 279)

metamorphic rock (met′ ə môr′ fik rok′) rock that forms when existing rock is changed by heat and pressure (p. 200)

migrate (mī′ grāt) to move to another place to find better climate, food, or a mate (p. 52)

mineral (min′ ər əl) natural material that forms from nonliving matter (p. 199)

mixture (miks′ chər) two or more kinds of matter that are placed together but can be easily separated (p. 306)

Moon (mün) the natural satellite that orbits around Earth (p. 432)

Moon phase (mün fāz) the way the Moon looks because of the amount of the lit side of the Moon that can be seen from Earth at the same time (p. 434)

motion (mō′shən) a change in the position of an object (p. 327)

natural resources (nach′ ər əl ri sôrs′əz) natural materials, such as soil, wood, water, air, oil, or minerals, that living things need (p. 247)

nonrenewable resources (non ri nü′ə bəl ri sôrs′ əz) resource that cannot be replaced once it is used up (p. 248)

nutrient (nü′ trē ənt) thing plants need in order to grow (p. 206)

observing (əb zėrv′ ing) using your senses to find out about objects, events, or living things (p. 4)

omnivore (om′ nə vôr′) living things that eat plants and other animals for food (p. 106)

orbit (ôr′ bit) the path of any object in space that revolves around another object in space (p. 456)

periodic table (pir′ē od′ik tā′bəl) an arrangement of elements based on their properties (p. 283)

physical change (fiz′ ə kəl chānj) a change that makes matter look different without becoming a new substance (p. 303)

pitch (pich) how high or low a sound is (p. 392)

planet (plan′it) a large body of matter that revolves, or travels, around any star (p. 456)

pollinate (pol′ ə nāt) move pollen from the part of a flower that makes pollen to the part of a flower that makes seeds (p. 15)

pollution (pə lü′ shən) waste materials that make the environment dirty (p. 124)

population (pop′ yə lā′ shən) all the living things of the same kind that live in the same place at the same time (p. 74)

position (pə zish′ ən) the location of an object (p. 327)

potential energy (pə ten′shəl en′ ər jē) the energy something has because of its position (p. 360)

precipitation (pri sip′ə tā′ shən) water that falls to Earth as rain, hail, sleet, or snow (p. 159)

predator (pred′ə tər) a consumer that hunts other animals for food (p. 107)

predicting (pri dikt′ ing) to tell what you think will happen (p. 162)

pressure (presh′ər) force per unit area that is applied to a substance (p. 281)

prey (prā) any animal that is hunted by others for food (p. 107)

producer (prə dü′sər) living things that make their own food (p. 106)

property (prop′ər tē) something about matter that you can observe with one or more of your senses (p. 279)

pulley (pùl′ē) a machine that changes the direction of motion of an object to which a force is applied (p. 343)

pupa (pyü′pə) stage in an insect's life between larva and adult (p. 45)

recycle (rē sī′kəl) treat or process something so it can be used again (p. 254)

reflect (ri flekt′) to bounce off of (p. 372)

refract (ri frakt′) to bend (p. 372)

relative position (rel′ə tiv pə zish′ən) a change in an object's position compared to another object (p. 329)

renewable resource (ri nü′ ə bəl ri sôrs′) resource that is endless like sunlight, or that is naturally replaced in a fairly short time, such as trees (p. 247)

resource (ri sôrs′) See Natural Resources, Renewable Resources, Nonrenewable Resources

revolution (rev′ə lü′ shən) one complete trip around the Sun (p. 428)

rock (rok) natural, solid, nonliving material made of one or more minerals (p. 199)

rotation (rō tā′ shən) one complete spin on an axis (p. 425)

scientific method (sī′ən tif′ik meth′əd) organized ways of finding answers and solving problems (p. xxvi)

sedimentary rock (sed′ə men′tər ē rok′) rock that forms when small pieces of earth materials collect and become bound together (p. 200)

seed leaf (sēd lēf) part of a seed that has stored food (p. 20)

seedling (sēd′ ling) a new, small plant that grows from a seed (p. 20)

sequence (sē′kwəns) the order in which events take place (p. 37, 221, 421, 477)

soil (soil) the part of Earth's surface consisting of humus and weathered rock in which plants grow (p. 206)

solid (sol′id) matter that has a definite shape and takes up a definite amount of space (p. 280)

solar system (sō′lər sis′təm) the Sun, the nine planets and their moons, and other objects that revolve around the Sun (p. 456)

solution (sə lü′shən) a mixture in which one or more substances dissolves in another (p. 308)

speed (spēd) the rate at which an object changes position (p. 330)

star (stär) a massive ball of hot gases that produces its own light (p. 423)

states of matter (stāts uv mat′ər) the forms of matter – solid, liquid, and gas (p. 304)

summarize (sum′ə rīz′) to cover the main ideas or details in a sentence or two (p. 325)

Sun (sun) our star; a huge ball of hot, glowing gases (p. 424)

system (sis′təm) a set of parts that interact with one another (p. 8)

technology (tek nol′ə jē) the use of science knowledge to invent tools and new ways of doing things (p. 479)

telescope (tel′ə skōp) a tool that gathers lots of light and magnifies objects that are far away and makes faint stars easier to see (p. 436)

thermal energy (thėr′məl en′ər jē) the total kinetic energy of all the particles that make up matter (p. 366)

tool (tül) an object used to do work (p. 479)

tornado (tôr nā′ dō) a rotating column of air that touches the ground and causes damage with its high winds (p. 182)

trait (trāt) a feature passed on to a living thing from its parents (p. 40)

tundra (tun′drə) land ecosystem that is cold and dry (p. 80)

vertebrate (vėr′tə brit) animal with a backbone (p. 40)

vibration (vī brā′shən) a very quick back-and-forth movement (p. 392)

volcano (vol kā′nō) an opening in the Earth's crust from which hot, melted material erupts (p. 226)

volume (vol′yəm) amount of space matter takes up (p. 285)

water cycle (wȯ′tər sī′kəl) the movement of water from Earth's surface into the air and back again (p. 158)

water vapor (wȯ′tər vā′pər) water in the form of an invisible gas in the air (p. 154)

weather (weŦH′ər) what it is like outside including temperature, wind, clouds, and precipitation (p. 175)

weathering (weŦH′ər ing) any process that changes rocks by breaking them into smaller pieces (p. 230)

wetland (wet′land′) low land ecosystem that is covered by water at least part of the time during the year; marshes and swamps are wetlands (p. 86)

wheel and axle (wēl and ak′səl) a simple machine made of a wheel and a rod joined to the center of the wheel (p. 342)

work (wėrk) what happens when a force moves an object over a distance (p. 338)

Index

This index lists the pages on which topics appear in this book. Page numbers after a *p* refer to a photograph or drawing. Page numbers after a *c* refer to a chart, graph, or diagram.

Rotation, *p*418, 424, *p*425, 428
of Earth, 425, 458, 459
of inner planets, 458
of Jupiter, 462
of Moon, 432, 433
of Neptune, 464
of Pluto, 465
of Uranus, 464

Rust, 311, *p*311

Saber tooth tiger, 55

Saguaro cactus, 181, *p*181

Salt, *c*205, 499, 508

Saltwater ecosystems, 88, *p*89

Sand in soil, 208, *p*208

Satellites, 484, *p*484, 496, *p*496

Saturn, 457, *p*457, 463, *p*463

Saxophone, *p*395

Science Fair Projects, 144, 272, 416, 512

Science Journal, 7, 13, 15, 17, 23, 39, 47, 57, 75, 82, 85, 89, 96, 103, 111, 115, 120, 161, 175, 183, 201, 204, 223, 233, 251, 279, 287, 309, 327, 333, 339, 359, 367, 369, 371, 373, 391, 385, 425, 431, 439, 461, 479, 481, 485, 489

Science Process Skills,
Classifying, 30, 132, 238, 244, 262, 406, 378, 379, 388, 414, 466

Collecting Data, 26, 27, 128, 129, 185, 211, 234, 258, 378, 379, 388, 414, 466

Communicating, 143, 271, 324, 356, 415, 511

Estimating and Measuring, 172, 210, 211, 269, 290, 291, 324, 356, 414, 415, 452, 511

Forming Questions and Hypotheses, 140, 268, 412, 508

Identifying and Controlling Variables, 140, 268, 508

Inferring, 30, 59, 62, 94, 100, 128, 129, 148, 162, 163, 166, 172, 188, 196, 215, 239, 259, 262, 276, 294, 300, 318, 345, 348, 382, 402, 403, 406, 407, 441, 444, 467, 499, 502

Interpreting Data, 26, 27, 90, 91, 94, 133, 184, 185, 235, 291,

Investigating and Experimenting, 268, 412, 508

Making and Using Models, 36, 196, 215, 220, 235, 238, 258, 440, 452, 466, 471, 498, 499, 508

Making Operational Definitions, 68

Observing, 4, 27, 58, 59, 68, 90, 100, 140, 163, 172, 211, 234, 258, 259, 268, 276, 300, 324, 344, 345, 356, 378, 379, 388, 402, 403, 420, 441, 476

Predicting, 62, 94, 133, 162, 166, 188, 215, 269, 276, 294, 314, 315, 318, 344, 345, 348, 382, 406, 412, 420

Scientific Methods for Experimenting, xxvi

Screw, 341, *p*341

Seagulls, *p*112

Sea jelly, 37, *c*42, *p*43

Seasons, *p*181, 428–429, 430, *c*431, *p*431
in Sonoran Desert, 181
start patterns and, 439

Seattle weather, *p*186, 186–187, *c*187

Sedimentary rock, *p*194, 200, 201, *p*201

Sedna, 465

Seed
in coniferous plant, 16, *p*17
in flowering plant, 15
germinating and growing, 20, 26–27
how do different kinds of seeds germinate?, 26–27, *c*27
making of, 15
parts of, *p*20
in pine cones, 19
releasing, 19
scattering, *p*18, 18–19

Seed cone, 16

Seed leaf, 2, *p*2, 20

Seedling, *p*3, 20, *p*21

Sequence, 37, 45, 51, 63, 221, 225, 229, *c*239, 239, 421, 423, 427, 429, 435, 445, 477, 491, 495, 503

Signal Words, 63

Sereno, Paul, 64

Credits

Photographs

Every effort has been made to secure permission and provide appropriate credit for photographic material. The publisher deeply regrets any omission and pledges to correct errors called to its attention in subsequent editions.

Unless otherwise acknowledged, all photographs are the property of Scott Foresman, a division of Pearson Education.

Photo locators denoted as follows: Top (T), Center (C), Bottom (B), Left (L), Right (R), Background (Bkgd).

Cover: ©Flip Nicklin/Minden Pictures, ©David Nardini/Getty Images.

Front Matter: iii Daniel J. Cox/Natural Exposures, (T) Getty Images; v ©Frans Lanting/Minden Pictures; vi ©DK Images; vii (R) ©Randy M. Ury/Corbis, (L) ©Breck P. Kent/Animals Animals/Earth Scenes; viii ©Jack Dykinga/Getty Images; xi ©Douglas Peebles/Corbis; xii ©Lloyd Cluff/Corbis; xv ©RNT Productions/Corbis; xxii ©Timothy O'Keefe/Index Stock Imagery; xxiii Getty Images; xxiv (Bkgd) ©Steve Bloom/Getty Images, (C) ©Robert Sullivan/AFP/Getty Images; xxix Getty Images; xxv ©Frank Greenaway/DK Images; xxviii (BL) Getty Images, (CL) ©Dave King/DK Images; xxx ©Comstock Inc.

Unit Dividers: Unit A (Bkgd) Getty Images, (CC) Digital Vision; Unit B (Bkgd) ©Kim Heacox/Getty Images, (BC) Getty Images; Unit C (Bkgd) ©Lester Lefkowitz/Getty Images; Unit D (Bkgd) Corbis

Chapter 1: 1 (B) ©Wolfgang Kaehler/Corbis, (T, C) Getty Images; 2 (T) ©John Warden/Index Stock Imagery, (BL) ©DK Images, (BL) Getty Images, ©Nigel Cattlin/Photo Researchers, Inc.; 3 (BL) ©Nigel Cattlin/Holt Studios, (BC) Neg./Transparency no. K13073. Courtesy Dept. of Library Services/American Museum of Natural History; 5 ©Stone/Getty Images, (Bkgd) ©John Warden/Index Stock Imagery; 6 ©John Warden/Index Stock Imagery; 7 (BR) ©Jim Steinberg/Photo Researchers, Inc., (TR) ©Photographer's Choice/Getty Images; 8 ©DK Images; 9 (CR, TR, BR) ©DK Images, (TC) Getty Images; 10 (R) Silver Burdett Ginn, (TL) Getty Images; 11 ©DK Images; 12 ©Lou Jacobs Jr./Grant Heilman Photography; 13 (TR) ©George Bernard/NHPA Limited, (TR) ©DK Images, (CR) ©TH Foto-Werbung/Photo Researchers, Inc., (TR) ©Niall Benvie/Corbis, (BR) ©The Garden Picture Library/Alamy Images; 14 (BL) ©Stone/Getty Images, (BR) ©Jeff Lepore/Photo Researchers, Inc., (TL) ©Peter Smithers/Corbis; 15 (BR) ©DK Images, (TL) Getty Images; 16 (B) ©Carolina Biological/Visuals Unlimited, (TL) Getty Images; 17 (CL) ©M & C Photography/Peter Arnold, Inc., (TR) ©Brad Mogen/Visuals Unlimited, (TC) ©Pat O'Hara/Corbis, (CR) ©Wally Eberhart/Visuals Unlimited, (BR) ©DK Images; 18 (BL) ©Darryl Torckler/Getty Images, (CC) ©Brian Gordon Green/NGS Image Collection, (BC) ©John Poutier/Maxx Images, Inc., (BC) ©Jorg & Petra Wegner/Animals Animals/Earth Scenes, (TL) ©DK Images; 19 (L) ©DK Images, (CR) ©Steve Bloom Images/Alamy Images; 21 (CL) ©DK Images, (CR) Nigel Cattlin/Holt Studios, (BC) ©Kenneth W. Fink/Photo Researchers, Inc., (BC) ©Nigel Cattlin/Photo Researchers, Inc.; 23 (TR) ©Dr. E. R. Degginger/Color-Pic, Inc., (CL) ©John Cancalosi/Peter Arnold, Inc., (TL) Neg./Transparency no. K13073. Courtesy Dept. of Library Services/American Museum of Natural History, (BR) ©David Muench/Muench

Photography, Inc, (CR) ©James L. Amos/Corbis; 24 (BL) ©The Natural History Museum, London, (BR, TL) DK Images; 26 ©Ed Young/Corbis; 28 (TR) ©Dennis MacDonald/PhotoEdit, (CR) ©Inga Spence/Visuals Unlimited, (CR) ©Steven Emery/Index Stock Imagery, (BR) ©Comstock Inc.; 31 (TL) ©DK Images, (TR) ©Kenneth W. Fink/Photo Researchers, Inc.; 32 (Bkgd) ©MSFC/NASA, (TL, BR) NASA; **Chapter 2:** 33 (B) ©Barbara Von Hoffmann/Animals Animals/Earth Scenes, (Bkgd) ©David Harrison/Index Stock Imagery; 34 (BL) ©David L. Shirk/Animals Animals/Earth Scenes, (T) ©Tom Brakefield/Corbis, (BR) ©Jeff L. Lepore/Photo Researchers, Inc.; 35 (BL, BR) ©Brad Mogen/Visuals Unlimited; 37 (C) ©David Stover/ImageState, (Bkgd) ©Tom Brakefield/Corbis; 38 ©Tom Brakefield/Corbis; 39 (BR) ©Tom Vezo/Nature Picture Library, (T) ©Zefa/Masterfile Corporation, (BL) ©Taxi/Getty Images, (BC) ©Natural Visions/Alamy Images, (TR) ©Frans Lanting/Minden Pictures; 40 (B) ©Tom Brakefield/Bruce Coleman Inc., (TL) ©Randy M. Ury/Corbis; 41 (CR) ©DK Images, (BC) ©Jim Brandenburg/Minden Pictures, (BR) ©Frans Lanting/Minden Pictures, (CR) Getty Images, (TR) ©Ken Lucas/Visuals Unlimited; 42 ©David Aubrey/Corbis; 43 (TR) ©Danny Lehman/Corbis, (TR) ©Robert Pickett/Corbis, (CR) ©The Image Bank/Getty Images, (BR) ©Brian Rogers/Visuals Unlimited; 44 (TL, TR) DK Images, (BR) ©Charles Melton/Visuals Unlimited; 45 (B) ©Brad Mogen/Visuals Unlimited, (T) ©Dick Scott/Visuals Unlimited; 46 (CL) ©Bettmann/Corbis, (BL) ©Keren Su/Photo Span/Alamy Images, (TL) ©Zefa/Masterfile Corporation; 47 (TR) ©Carolina Biological Supply Company/Phototake, (CL, BL) ©DK Images, (TL) ©Breck P. Kent/Animals Animals/Earth Scenes, (BR) ©Randy M. Ury/Corbis; 48 (BR) ©DK Images, (TR) ©Ken Lucas/Visuals Unlimited, (TL) ©Tony Evans/Timelapse Library/Getty Images; 49 (TL) ©Frans Lanting/Minden Pictures, (TR) ©Kevin Schafer/Corbis, (CR) ©Gary W. Carter/Corbis, (BR) ©DK Images; 50 ©Vittoriano Rastelli/Corbis, (TL) ©Photodisc Green/Getty Images; 51 (TC) ©Rod Planck/Photo Researchers, Inc., (CC) ©James Robinson/Animals Animals/Earth Scenes, (TL) ©Michael Quinton/Minden Pictures, (TR) ©Chris Newbert/Minden Pictures, (CL) ©The Image Bank/Getty Images, (BL) ©Rolf Kopfle/Bruce Coleman Inc., (BC) ©Tim Laman/NGS Image Collection, (BC) ©Suzanne L. & Joseph T. Collins/Photo Researchers, Inc., (CC) ©Steve E. Ross/Photo Researchers, Inc., (TC) ©Ken Wilson/Papilio/Corbis, (CR) ©David Aubrey/Corbis, (BR) ©E. R. Degginger/Bruce Coleman, Inc., (BL) ©Rick & Nora Bowers/Visuals Unlimited; 52 (TR) ©DK Images, (BR) ©George Grall/NGS Image Collection, (BR) ©Jeff L. Lepore/Photo Researchers, Inc., (TL) ©Eric and David Hosking/Corbis, (TL) ©Photodisc Blue/Getty Images; 53 (T) ©Gerry Ellis/Minden Pictures, (B) ©Terry W. Eggers/Corbis; 54 (TL) ©James L. Amos/Photo Researchers, Inc., (B) ©DK Images, (CL) ©Layne Kennedy/Corbis; 55 (TL) ©DK Images, (TR) ©Breck P. Kent/Animals Animals/Earth Scenes; 56 (R) ©Breck P. Kent/Animals Animals/Earth Scenes, Senekenberg Nature Museum/©DK Images, (TL) Colin Keates/Courtesy of the Natural History Museum, London/©DK Images; 57 ©Ross M. Horowitz/Getty Images; 58 ©Larry L. Miller/Photo Researchers, Inc.; 60 Digital Vision; 61 ©Masa Ushioda/Visual & Written/Bruce Coleman, Inc.; 63 ©DK Images; 64 (TL) ©Dutheil Didier/SYGMA/Corbis, (BL) ©Reuters/Corbis; **Chapter 3:** 65 (Bkgd) Getty Images, (T) ©Photodisc Green/Getty Images; 66 (T) ©Mark E. Gibson Stock Photography, (BL) ©J. Eastcott/Y. Eastcott Film/NGS Image Collection, (BR) ©Enzo & Paolo Ragazzini/Corbis; 67 (BL) ©Andy Binns/Ecoscene, (BR)

©Jim Zipp/Photo Researchers, Inc., (CR) ©Alan Carey/Photo Researchers, Inc., (TR) ©Steve Kaufman/Corbis; 69 ©Mark E. Gibson Stock Photography; 70 ©Mark E. Gibson Stock Photography; 71 ©Siede Preis/Getty Images; 72 Getty Images; 73 (Bkgd) ©Melissa Farlow/Aurora & Quanta Productions, (TC) ©DK Images, (BC) ©Kurt Stier/Corbis; 74 (CL) ©Royalty-Free/Corbis, (BL) ©Alan Carey/Photo Researchers, Inc.; 75 (CR) ©Joseph Van Os/Getty Images, (L) ©Kennan Ward/Corbis, (BR) Darren Bennett/Animals Animals/Earth Scenes; 76 ©OSF/Animals Animals/Earth Scenes; 77 (T) ©Enzo & Paolo Ragazzini/Corbis, (BL) ©Jason Edwards/NGS Image Collection, (BR) ©Steve Kaufman/Corbis; 78 (BL) ©Jack Dykinga/Getty Images, (BR) Jerry Young/©DK Images, (T) ©DK Images; 79 (Bkgd) ©J. Eastcott/Y. Eastcott Film/NGS Image Collection, (TL) Daniel J. Cox/Natural Exposures; 80 (BL) Daniel J. Cox/Natural Exposures, (TL) ©Ed Reschke/Peter Arnold, Inc.; 81 (L) ©Andy Binns/Ecoscene, (TR, CL, CR) Daniel J. Cox/Natural Exposures; 82 ©Tim Laman/NGS Image Collection; 83 (TR) ©Michio Hoshino/Minden Pictures, (TL, BR) ©Jim Brandenburg/Minden Pictures, (BL) ©Jay Dickman/Corbis, (CR) ©David Ulmer/Stock Boston; 84 (CR) ©Roy Toft/NGS Image Collection, (TR) ©Claus Meyer/Minden Pictures, (BR) ©Ken Preston-Mafham/Animals Animals/Earth Scenes, (TL) Alamy; 85 (BL) ©Michael & Patricia Fogden/Minden Pictures, (T) ©Tui De Roy/Minden Pictures; 86 (B) Daniel J. Cox/Natural Exposures, (TL) ©Roy Toft/NGS Image Collection; 87 (Bkgd) Daniel J. Cox/Natural Exposures, (TR) ©Joseph H. Bailey/NGS Image Collection; 88 (TL) ©Medford Taylor/NGS Image Collection, (BR) ©Fred Bavendam/Peter Arnold, Inc.; 89 (TR) ©Mick Turner/PhotoLibrary, (Bkgd) ©Royalty-Free/Corbis; 90 Getty Images; 95 ©Ken Preston-Mafham/Animals Animals/Earth Scenes; 96 ©Bettmann/Corbis. **Chapter 4:** 97 ©M. Colbeck/OSF/Animals Animals/Earth Scenes; 98 (T) ©Stephen Frink/Corbis, (BL) ©Carol Havens/Corbis, (BR) ©K. H. Haenel/Zefa/Masterfile Corporation; 99 (T) ©D. Robert and Lorri Franz/Corbis, (TR) ©Jim Brandenburg/Minden Pictures, (CR) ©Dr. Gopal Murti/Photo Researchers, Inc., (BR) ©Gerald Hinde/ABPL/Animals Animals/Earth Scenes; 101 (CR) ©Richard Walters/Visuals Unlimited, (Bkgd) ©Stephen Frink/Corbis, (BR) ©Bob Marsh/Papilio/Corbis, (CC) ©David Boag/Alamy Images; 102 ©Stephen Frink/Corbis; 103 (CR) Brand X Pictures, (BR) ©Patti Murray/Earth Scenes/Maxx Images, Inc., (CR) ©Laura Sivell/Papilio/Corbis, (TR) Getty Images; 104 (B) ©Richard Kolar/Animals Animals/Earth Scenes, (T) ©Rick Raymond/Index Stock Imagery; 105 (T) ©Michael & Patricia Fogden/Corbis, (B) ©B. Jones/M. Shimlock/Photo Researchers, Inc.; 106 (BL) ©Chase Swift/Corbis, (BC) ©Carol Havens/Corbis, (BR) ©Frank Blackburn/Ecoscene/Corbis, (TL) ©Hope Ryden/NGS Image Collection; 107 (B) ©D. Robert and Lorri Franz/Corbis, (T) ©K. H. Haenel/Zefa/Masterfile Corporation, (CR) ©Randy Wells/Corbis, (BL) ©Danny Lehman/Corbis; 108 (TL, BL) Getty Images, (BR) ©Yva Momatiuk/John Eastcott/Minden Pictures, (BC) ©Naturfoto Honal/Corbis, (CC) ©Kevin R. Morris/Corbis; 109 (C) Minden Pictures, (R) ©Claudia Adams/Alamy Images, (BL) ©Tom Brakefield/Corbis; 110 (TL) ©Gerry Ellis/Minden Pictures, (CL) ©Michael & Patricia Fogden/Corbis, (BL) ©Martin Harvey/Photo Researchers, Inc., (TL) ©Photodisc Green/Getty Images; 111 ©Gerald Hinde/ABPL/Animals Animals/Earth Scenes; 112 (TL) ©DK Images, (CL) ©Raymond Gehman/Corbis, (BL) ©Scott Camazine/Photo Researchers, Inc.; 113 ©Paal Hermansen/

EM28